Praise for Egypt Sherrod and *Keep Calm . . . It's Just Real Estate*

"Egypt Sherrod is my Realtor BFF in my head and *Keep Calm . . . It's Just Real Estate* should be a MUST HAVE for all buyers. I wish I read this book when I was buying my first property."

**—Stacy London,
television host and author**

"This book is just what the doctor ordered! It's just like Egypt to want to make everyone's life easier and simplify the stressful buying and selling process. *Keep Calm . . . It's Just Real Estate* gives you all the tools needed to come out smiling and on TOP."

**—Keke Wyatt,
recording artist and star of TV One's *R&B Divas***

"Egypt has a knack for helping buyers figure out what really matters to them, and then coming up with a plan to make it happen. When the hunt gets overwhelming, Egypt puts things into perspective. Having her on your side is like having a BFF who's a real estate pro. Now she's captured all of that wisdom in a book, so every reader can go house-shopping with confidence."

**—Betsy Riley, executive editor,
Atlanta Magazine's Home edition**

"Flawless but simple execution should always be the objective of every real estate transaction. Egypt is a professional who is laser-focused on getting the transaction right the first time. This drive is what sets her apart, and it's well-reflected in her book."

**—Lisa Brereton-Hinds,
Vice President of Starkey M**

KEEP CALM... IT'S JUST REAL ESTATE

YOUR NO-STRESS GUIDE TO BUYING A HOME

by **EGYPT SHERROD**

host of *Property Virgins*

with Amber Noble Garland

RUNNING PRESS
PHILADELPHIA · LONDON

Books published by Running Press are available at special discounts for bulk purchases in the United States by corporations, institutions, and other organizations. For more information, please contact the Special Markets Department at the Perseus Books Group, 2300 Chestnut Street, Suite 200, Philadelphia, PA 19103, or call (800) 810-4145, ext. 5000, or e-mail special.markets@perseusbooks.com.

ISBN 978-0-7624-5755-7
Library of Congress Control Number: 2014959820

E-book ISBN 978-0-7624-5756-4

9 8 7 6 5 4 3 2 1
Digit on the right indicates the number of this printing

Cover design by Frances Soo Ping Chow
Interior design by Amanda Richmond
Edited by Jennifer Kasius
Typography: Chronicle and Verlag.

Running Press Book Publishers
2300 Chestnut Street
Philadelphia, PA 19103-4371

Visit us on the web!
www.runningpress.com

This book is dedicated to my amazing daughter,
Kendall, who has given my life true purpose.
You are my reason why. Mommy is doing it all for you.

✳✳✳

To my wonderful husband, Mike.
As the saying goes, "We've come a long way baby."

✳✳✳

Immense gratitude to my prayer warriors who keep me covered at
all times, thank you for your loyalty and love. I am truly blessed.

CONTENTS

✳✳✳

INTRODUCTION . . . 8

CHAPTER 1

BUYING A HOME WITH CONFIDENCE:
Ready to Take the Plunge? . . . 14

CHAPTER 2

BUILDING YOUR
REAL ESTATE DREAM TEAM:
The First Step . . . 29

CHAPTER 3

DON'T WORRY, BUY HAPPY!
Finding the Home of Your Dreams . . . 47

CHAPTER 4

DISTRESSED PROPERTIES:
Are They Really Worth the Hunt? . . . 65

CHAPTER 5

THE DOWN AND DIRTY
ABOUT DOWNPAYMENTS:
Knowing What You Can Afford . . . 80

CHAPTER 6

GETTING APPROVED
FOR A MORTGAGE:
Which Home Loan Is Right for You? . . . 88

CHAPTER 7

THE THRILL OF MAKING AN OFFER:
How to Seal the Deal . . . 110

CHAPTER 8

GET OUT YOUR MAGNIFYING GLASS:
Why You Should Never Overlook the Inspection . . . 123

CHAPTER 9

APPRAISALS:
Comps, Reports, Results . . . Oh My! . . . 140

CHAPTER 10

COMMON PITFALLS TO AVOID:
Home Buying No No's . . . 147

CHAPTER 11

THE TITLE SCRUB DOWN:
Not All Title Companies Are Created Equal . . . 157

CHAPTER 12

THE CLOSING TABLE:
The Final Frontier . . . 169

CHAPTER 13

UNLOCKING THE DOORS OF YOUR NEW HOME:
Now What? . . . 178

GLOSSARY

THE LINGO
Real Estate Terms to Know . . . 185

ACKNOWLEDGMENTS . . . 213

INDEX . . . 215

INTRODUCTION

BUYING OR SELLING A HOUSE CAN BE JUST AS PER-plexing as deciding which hand to keep or discard at a casino. But it doesn't have to be. If you make the right decisions early on, put a great team in place, and follow the instructions I give you in this book, you will feel like a pro playing among the card sharks in no time!

To win at anything, you have to fully understand the game, or at the very least, have a team that does. In real estate, the game is not just about choosing the right home. It comes down to strategy, assessment, planning, organization, and skill. If that sounds like a heavy load, don't worry, you don't have to go it alone. The weight can be carried by finding the right professionals to help you through the home-buying process. Having experts guide you will garner better results than trying to do it all yourself. For starters, utilizing experienced real estate professionals will save you time and money, and will help you avoid unnecessary hassles.

For those of you who yearn to understand the perceived "mysteries" behind successful real estate deals, you've come to the right place. I happen to be just the person who will be able to demystify the real estate buying and selling process, ultimately making it much simpler for you to understand. I will teach you how to pick the winners instead of the losers. Well, maybe not in a game of spades, bridge, or UNO, but certainly in regard to real estate.

Here's a little about me before you begin reading: I am a realtor licensed in two states—and have been an agent since 2003. My business partner and I have sold over $50 million in properties. I personally enjoy working with first-time homebuyers, and you can watch me doing just that on my highly rated HGTV show *Property Virgins*. It brings me personal joy to help families achieve the American Dream of homeownership.

When I was twenty-four years old, I purchased my first property. It was overwhelming, confusing, and exciting all at the same time. Ask any millionaire, and he or she will tell you that the foundation of wealth is real estate. I knew that I was making the right decision by purchasing versus renting, but the nuances and paperwork made my head spin. My uncle had been a real estate broker for over thirty years, so I had more knowledge than the average "Property Virgin." Still, I was intimidated just by the thought of what I imagined the process entailed.

Don't laugh, but the moment I got the keys to my first property, I cried like a baby. In that minute, I realized I owned a piece of the earth. Land is one thing we can never make more of. It is what it is on this earth, and I actually owned my own little piece of it. It was such an exhilarating feeling, and I was hooked. By the time I was thirty, I had flipped more than a dozen investment properties, earning a hefty profit. As time went on and market conditions changed, I decided that buying and holding made more long-term sense for me. There is no doubt in my mind that owning real estate can help you build substantial wealth—if it's done correctly.

Like starting a new relationship, many people go about their real estate ventures the wrong way. They fall in love with the exterior, but underneath the cosmetic enhancements and curb appeal can lie structural defects that may alter the building's integrity. Often there might be material defects connected to the home that you don't learn about until after you've signed on the dotted line and are stuck with a thirty-year mortgage. Sound familiar? I pray not! My hope is that I have caught your interest in time, *before* you embark upon the joys of homeownership and so you don't make costly mistakes. Knowledge not only gives you power, but it also gives you the extra edge to make smarter decisions regarding the purchase of a new home. After all, you're going to live in it for a while, so you'd better like it!

Along the way on your quest toward homeownership, you may make mistakes. Keep calm . . . it's okay! This book will help Property Virgins, but it will also help those who may be recovering from a bad experience in buying or selling a home, and who simply want to make better decisions going forward.

Take for example, first-time buyer Natasha, a pharmaceutical sales rep from Boston. She received a job promotion that required her to relocate to Florida in a hurry. After scouting several homes online, this impatient cash-buyer eventually found one that suited all of her needs. But before dipping her feet in the water to purchase it, Natasha asked a friend to preview the home in person on her behalf.

After Natasha finally got into her new home and started unpacking, she awoke several times throughout the night to the loudest noise she had ever heard. It sounded like a freight train coming through the house. As it turned out, there were train tracks just a few hundred yards away from her home. Three or four times per hour, a l-o-o-o-n-n-g-g-g cargo train went by and shook the whole house! Her friend had no way of knowing this when he viewed the property. He was inexperienced and didn't necessarily know the right questions to ask or the red flags to look out for. Not to mention, the real estate agent showing the property was a "listing agent," or "seller's agent." That meant that the agent's primary responsibility was to the seller, not the buyer! Although the agent was not dishonest—she did mention on the phone that there was a train nearby that ran only "a couple of times a day." In actuality, she did not know much about the train schedule and had just made a wild guess.

In hindsight, Natasha should have hired a real estate "buyer's agent" familiar with the area to work on her behalf. That agent may have pointed out details that the seller's agent left out.

Natasha also should have hired a specialized real estate attorney who was familiar with Florida laws to carefully review her contract and closing documents. Instead, the Boston-based buyer trusted the "friend," who was not familiar with the laws in Florida, where she was purchasing. The paperwork wound up being a headache, and the whole home-buying experience was a giant fiasco.

Fast forward nine months. Natasha was astounded to discover the home she just paid cash for was plagued by a "dirty title" that was riddled with blemishes and liens against the property. The sum of these mishaps caused her great distress and anxiety, ultimately leading Natasha to regret her decision to buy the home. Certainly, any costly setback can ruin the joys of owning a home very quickly!

Everything becomes simpler when you understand it, because education is the key to success in anything we do. Purchasing real estate is no different than learning anything else new for the first-time. You may be a home-buying newbie, such as a young couple or a single person who is simply tired of paying rent. Perhaps you've been renting and now want a place of your own so you can provide stability and comfort for your family. Maybe you are someone who is skeptical about buying another home due to a past negative experience. Whatever your circumstance, keep calm, because now you have me to be your personal real estate guide.

After you read this book, I recommend that you keep it within arm's reach, perhaps stowed in a handy compartment of your vehicle. Then you will always have me with you if you need a quick reference or reminder as you go through the home-buying process. Within the pages of *Keep Calm . . . It's Just Real Estate*, you will find no-holds-barred, real answers.

As a real estate agent, owner, and investor, I have ridden the emotional roller coaster of the housing industry and fared just fine. I have soared to the heights of success, and I have counted my beans when the market hit bottom. I persisted, and I made it because real estate is my passion. I truly enjoy helping people find the home of their dreams, but even more so, I find serenity in knowing that I can provide my clients with guidance and answers in an industry that can be confusing and complicated to those who are not familiar with how the process works.

So with that said, if you are ready to learn how to swim in the real estate shark tank, dive in! I'll catch you (or at least swim beside you). And if you commit to following the guidelines that I offer in this book, and keep in mind the prescriptive "Chill Pills" I note in each chapter, then you will surely backstroke through the home-buying process in no time!

CHAPTER 1

BUYING A HOME WITH CONFIDENCE:
Ready to Take the Plunge?

IF THE THOUGHT OF BITING INTO YOUR OWN PIECE of the real estate pie makes you feel anxious or nervous, fear not! This is perfectly normal. After all, this definitely qualifies as a "major life decision," and will go down in your personal history book of awesome accomplishments one day.

Once you decide to buy, go forward with confidence and let the goodness flow to you. The way to do this begins by choosing the right guidance and support team, trusting your instincts, using all the common sense you can muster up, and focusing on the most important aspects of what you want in a home. For example, you may have to sacrifice a few vanity items in order to gain something else that could pay off handsomely in the long run. You may even have to let go of some personal or emotional attachments to be able to live in a certain location, or let go of your preferred style of home to buy something within your means. In other words, the first lesson in home-buying is this: **Be flexible!**

I emphasize flexibility because I've had numerous clients who fall head over heels in love with a house, but hesitate because their dresser wouldn't fit in the bedroom. Or, they don't have a table long enough for the massive dining room in the new house. Furniture will always be replaceable. It is much more difficult to find the perfect house versus the perfect sofa. Don't be so rigid that you miss an opportunity, but by the same token, don't settle for a home that you have to work really hard to convince yourself you like.

There is a difference between focusing on what really matters versus letting your head turn toward cosmetic qualities. For example, I once had a realtor friend who showed a couple at least ten homes and condominiums before they settled on one they liked. Finally, they signed the paperwork for a gorgeous townhome. After living there for only a month or so, everything started falling apart! Shoddy materials were used when the contractors built the townhomes, so although the home was only a couple of years old, there were minor things that constantly cost them money and time to repair. It was a "money pit" with unexpected pitfalls. Closet doors mysteriously fell off the hinges with very little encouragement; the toilet latch no longer flushed properly, there were small cracks in the wall where the foundation had settled; and the windows never shut properly. Needless to say, the heat and their money flew right out the window. These constant hassles made the place not-so-appealing after just a few weeks.

Structural details are the most vital and lasting aspects of a home. Be careful not to get so enamored by the way a place looks on the surface that you overlook the most important factors. As they say, "Looks fade!" and this holds true with real estate.

ARE YOU READY TO TAKE A LEAP OF FAITH?

When shopping for a home, you should be mindful of those you accept advice from and whether they are qualified to give it to you. Do they have a vested interest in you purchasing the property? Family members and friends are usually the ones inadvertently giving poor advice when it comes to real estate. Market conditions are constantly fluctuating. Additionally, the housing climate can vary from state to state. So you may be getting outdated or jaded advice. **Rule of thumb: Listen to the experts!**

Of course, if you are married or in a partnership with someone who will be sharing homeownership, you should be conscious of what your individual and combined goals are. The purchase of a house is probably one of the biggest and most important decisions you will make, especially with a partner. Go into it with a clear mind and both feet firmly planted. Don't allow yourself to be talked into something you are uncomfortable with or unprepared for. Don't let yourself be rushed through the process if you're not ready.

CHILL PILL #2

Take real estate advice strictly from the professionals. Family and friends mean well but can give you bad information. Consult with a qualified real estate professional who has the experience to back up their advice—and who can offer you an impartial perspective as an outsider.

You may still be wondering if you are even ready to buy a house. There are a lot of factors to consider: your personal finances, whether your job will stay where you are, whether you can afford to buy in the neighborhood where you'd like to live. Only you can decide if homeownership is the right step for you. But by the time you finish this book, you'll have the proper information and tools to make an educated choice and move forward with confidence.

Consider the following ten things first. If you respond favorably to most of them—let's say seven out of the ten—then you may indeed be a terrific candidate for owning your own home.

TOP TEN THINGS TO CONSIDER
BEFORE BUYING A HOME

1. Given your particular circumstances, how long would you see yourself living in your new home? Five years? Ten? Longer? If your answer is five years or more, then buying real estate is a smart move, since the money you will spend every year on rent is only making your landlord wealthy for the long term.

2. Would you be doing it for the right reasons? Would you be purchasing because it's a personal goal? Or is this someone else's goal for your life? Outside pressure should not be a factor. Buying a house can cause some anxiety, yes, but ideally you will find joy in the process. If you feel good about wanting a home of your own, then that is the right feeling to have!

3. What does your financial picture look like? Do you have a significant down payment saved up? One lesson learned by so many millions of homeowners within the past few years is that the "no money down" method was a disaster. Banks are more cautious than ever, and most prefer having at least 20 percent of the purchase price as a down payment. Lucky for you, there are many first-time homebuyer programs that will allow you to put as little as 3–3.5 percent down. You can find more about this in my chapter on mortgages.

4. Do you have a financial contingency plan or back up in case something happens? After shelling out the down payment, you don't want to be caught using up your last resources in case your water heater breaks, or your roof starts to leak. Make sure your investment is sound, but plan ahead! You should also make a solid spreadsheet to determine your monthly expenses and budget. Be organized to make sure you won't get hit with late fees from the bank or be overrun by high utility bills, which can really tap into your resources and make homeownership a stressful experience.

5. How sure are you about your job? If your job is unsteady or if you have been in your workplace for less than five years, make sure your position is stable. Of course life can dish out surprises ("Want to tranfer to Hong Kong?"), but if you know that you will be able to manage and that you are making enough to sustain your lifestyle, then buying a house can be done with peace of mind.

6. Are you willing to make sacrifices? Having your own house means that you will be responsible if something breaks or needs repair. You can't call up your landlord and ask for it to be fixed. You will either have to do these things yourself or hire someone. That also includes landscaping and other maintenance tasks that are often covered for you when you rent.

7. New or used? Although some people like to start from scratch and build a home on a piece of land, most homes are bought from a previous owner—or multiple owners.

Consider whether or not you have the time, dedication, and will to build a home, or if you prefer the joys of renovating.

8. Are you being realistic? You may wish to live by the ocean, but perhaps your budget only enables you to live in a neighborhood with a pond nearby. Don't overstretch your means, even if you fall in love with something better than your initial comfort zone. Some pushy agents may attempt to show you properties that are more expensive than what you planned, but if you keep a realistic outlook and stay focused on your comfort zone, you can request only to see homes that fall within your specific criteria.

9. In addition to your down payment, there will be costs such as closing fees, real estate attorney fees, title fees, and even the cost of moving. Can you afford the up-front costs?

10. Finally, what do you need the home to give you to make this feel like a worthwhile investment? If you plan to live there for less than five years, then my recommendation is to reconsider buying. It can often take five years or longer to recoup the money that you pay in closing costs. Oh my goodness . . . did I just say, *"Don't buy?"* Those words are blasphemy coming out of a real estate agent's mouth. Nevertheless, truth is truth!

It may be wise to make a list of all the pros and cons to buying a home. If there are downsides that will take time to overcome (like not having enough for a down payment), then make a game plan before jumping in with both feet.

But for those of you who are tired of living under someone else's rules, having to deal with thin walls, unpredictable neighbors, and throwing hard-earned rent money away, the prospect of owning a home might be a dream come true. In most cases, it is!

WHY ARE YOU MAKING YOUR LANDLORD RICH?

My personal belief is that when you rent, you make your landlord rich. It's simple math. Add up your rent and multiply it by twelve. You will be amazed at just how much you are padding that landlord's account! So whenever it makes the most sense, BUY! At least eight times out of ten, it makes more sense to buy your own house instead of renting and having nothing to show after years of paying.

Wouldn't you rather establish financial security for yourself? Nowadays, rentals are just about equal with what a mortgage payment would cost (though you shouldn't discount the extras, like paying for your own maintenance and utilities and property taxes).

People have a number of reasons why they decide to rent versus buy. Their reasons vary wildly depending on their own personal circumstances or life scenarios. Most of these have very little connection with the possibilities of homeownership, or whether the person can actually afford a home. Here are the most common objections I hear:

- I've lived in an apartment my entire life and just never thought I could be a candidate for homeownership. (*Well surprise!!! You certainly can.*)

- I screwed up my credit up when I was younger. I'm sure no bank will finance me, so why bother? (*Credit scores fluctuate all the time. Debts you incurred five years ago may no longer be on your credit report. But you won't know until you at least try.*)

- No one in my family has ever owned a home, so I didn't think I could be an owner. (*Why not be the first? Set an example for the rest of your family and future generations. When they see how you managed to accomplish owning a home, it may encourage them to do the same.*)

- Owning seems so much more expensive than renting. (*Aha! That's a big misconception. Many times a mortgage works out to be cheaper than paying rent. Additionally, you get tax incentives for homeownership. AND when you sell your home, for the most part you get your investment back and then some. Renting works out to be much more expensive in the long run.*)

- I just don't want all of the responsibilities that come with owning a home. (*Well, there is a point I cannot rebut. If you're not ready, you're not ready.*)

These are all valid and understandable concerns. However, they should not be deterrents. Everyone has hurdles to overcome, but if you do as you've always done, you'll only get what you've always gotten. It's easy to make excuses that allow you to stay in a comfort zone. Sometimes we have to force ourselves to be uncomfortable in order to grow.

This reminds me of my personal experience of landing the job as host of *Property Virgins*. At the time, I was a full-time real estate agent in New Jersey and a full-time radio personality in New York. I knew my plate was already full when I received a call from a casting agent who wanted me to fly to Toronto for an audition. Within the first minute after he mentioned it, I had already thought of ten good reasons why I shouldn't go. *"I'll waste my time flying there because they probably already have another host in mind. I'll have to take three days off my radio show, which my boss will frown at. Better yet, if he finds out I took off to go on an audition, I'll probably get fired."* I mean, you name it, and I already said it to myself. But then a little voice inside said, *"You are a great real estate agent, so why wouldn't they pick you? Give yourself a break. You said you wanted to get back into television hosting, and now is your opportunity. Take a chance on yourself."*

Well, I took that chance, bet on myself, and today not only do I get to educate viewers on a huge international platform about the wonders of owning real estate, but I also got to write this book and personally help *you*! It's all because I dared to follow my dream and did the work to get there. I believe you can and will do it, too.

THE REAL ESTATE REWIND:
LET'S RECAP!

Use these three gauges to determine whether buying a home may make more sense than renting a place to live:

- If you are looking for stability and long-term wealth, then it makes absolute sense to buy, especially with mortgage interest rates still sitting at record lows. Many mortgage payments are coming in lower than rent.

- Be sure to consider the total cost of homeownership beyond the monthly mortgage payment. Plan for your down payment, plus 3 to 5 percent more for closing costs. Maintenance will run an average of 1 percent of your home's price every year. Make sure you don't forget insurance and property taxes, but keep your eyes on the prize; the upside is the biggest deduction on your yearly taxes.

- Finally, ask yourself if you really want to be a homeowner. Are you the type of person who enjoys weekly trips to a home improvement store, or would you rather just call your landlord to come fix your squeaky floorboard? Do you mind moving around every two years, or would you prefer to set down long-term roots?

LIST OF 12 PROS
FOR PROPERTY VIRGINS

Only you can decide if the path to homeownership is the one you should take. But here are twelve fantastic benefits to becoming a homeowner that you may not have thought of:

1. **Wealth Building:** Real estate is a vital asset in building a foundation of wealth for your family. Some people who own their property for an extended period of time are surprised to see how much the value increases with each decade.

2. **Better Management:** Many people fail to call their land-lord when something breaks—or their landlord fails to make requested repairs—both of which leads to rentals that are in disrepair. When you own your own home, the expenses to pay for repairs will come out of your own pocket, but the benefit is in your ability to be in absolute control of your home's upkeep and make it a beautiful, reliable place to live.

3. **Credit Score:** Making those monthly payments to the mortgage company in a timely fashion will eventually give you great marks on your credit score. A mortgage in good standing improves credit scores by leaps and bounds.

4. Tax Breaks: The US Tax Code lets you deduct the interest you pay on your mortgage, property taxes, and certain costs associated with buying your home.

5. Appreciation: Real estate has long-term, stable growth in value. While year-to-year fluctuations are normal, median existing-home sale prices increased on average 6.5 percent each year from 1972 through 2005. Because of the economy, we bottomed out for a few years 2006 to 2012. But the economy is back on track, and so are the benefits of owning real estate. In addition, the number of US households is expected to rise 15 percent over the next decade, creating continued high demand for housing.

6. Stability: If you plan on having a family—or if you have one already—owning a home is a great benefit to your children. They like having a place of comfort to call "home" and often feel a palpable difference between places that are "theirs" versus places that are rented. Stability is essential to children, so take their well-being and feelings into account when you make your decision.

7. Equity: Money paid for rent is money that you'll never see again, but mortgage payments let you build equity ownership interest in your home. Although the average rent varies depending on which state or region you live in, if you were paying $1,200 per month in rent for a two- or three-bedroom apartment, single-family home, or condo, then you can kiss that $14,400 per year, good-bye forever, whereas, that money applied to a mortgage will go toward the principal. You will be another year closer to owning your home, rather than wasting another year of your hard-earned money to pay the landlord's mortgage.

8. **Predictability**: Unlike rent, your fixed-mortgage payments won't increase over the years, so your housing costs may actually decline the longer you own your home. However, bear in mind that property taxes and insurance costs will increase.

9. **Pride:** Having a home can give you a sense of fulfillment and achievement. You have something you can be proud of—your own little piece of the earth!

10. **Community:** When you have your own house, it gives you a chance to bond with neighbors and other people in the neighborhood. They come to know you and vice versa, so you'll have more eyes to help you look out for your house in case of danger. When you rent, it can be difficult to get to know people because renters are known for fluttering from one place to the next.

11. **Pets:** Having pets is a hassle when you rent. Aside from the extra deposit that is almost always required, there is the fear of damage to the property. When you own a house, you don't need to ask permission to have a dog or a cat.

12. Freedom: The home is yours. You can decorate any way you like and benefit from your investment for as long as you own the home. You'll never have to ask permission to build a deck, install a dish on your roof, change the carpet to hardwood flooring, or worry about your landlord stopping by unexpectedly after your children just turned the place upside down. It's your place! You can do as you wish . . . well, almost. Sans a homeowners association. More on this in my chapter on HOA's.

Homeownership is a commitment. Once you know you want that commitment, and you're sure it's right for you, then you can move forward and take the right steps to get into that house of your dreams. If you're ready, let's take that first step!

CHAPTER 2

BUILDING YOUR REAL ESTATE DREAM TEAM:
The First Step

GREAT, YOU TURNED THE PAGE! I GUESS THAT MEANS you're ready for the nitty gritty. Let's talk about building your team. The quarterback and MVP of your real estate dream team will be your agent. A qualified and experienced agent will easily be able to advise you on the other members you will need to add to your roster, such as the inspector and attorney. We'll cover those key positions in later chapters.

Having been a real estate agent for over a dozen years, I have consistently done my very best for all of my clients. But I didn't learn to be a fantastic agent on my own. Hats off to the many stellar agents I have met and worked with over the years! A few of them helped me perfect my craft and grow my business by teaching me the most valuable qualities of a good agent. If your agent does not possess the following traits, then you should consider seeking the services of another. If you are planning on buying or selling a home soon, this advice can save you a lot of time, grief, and money.

FOUR QUALITIES OF EXCELLENT AGENTS

- **Commitment:** Ability to focus their complete time and attention on you and your needs.

- **Communication**: Ability to listen and respond to what you want, not just what they want to sell you.

- **Ambition**: Have a willingness to go the extra mile to help you find the right home or to sell a listing.

- **Integrity**: Putting honesty and ethics before any personal gain.

These are the essential characteristics, my friends! No matter how many millions of dollars in sales an agent had last year—or whether they were the top realtor in their office, won all kinds of sales awards, promised to work hard for you, or even if they look like Brad Pitt or Angelina Jolie—none of these qualities make them a great realtor! Remember, with commitment, communication, ambition, and integrity, you can't go wrong!

> ## CHILL PILL #3
>
> Vet your realtor! This is one of the biggest purchases you'll make in your lifetime. It's important that the person representing you is qualified and experienced enough to do the job effectively. You deserve the best, so make sure you hire the best.

Sadly, after the housing crisis of 2007 to 2009 consumer confidence hit an all-time low. Anyone working in any aspect of the real estate business was perceived to be culpable for the disaster. But, the truth is, real estate agents had nothing to do with the bottom falling out of the market.

Nowadays, because of the uncertainty about who can be trusted, many buyers think they're doing themselves a favor if they avoid sticking to one real estate agent. Instead, they bounce around to multiple agents or simply go off on their own to try to find a house to buy. They scour the internet or drive around neighborhoods, which is both time consuming and not the most efficient way to go about finding the best property to suit your needs and desires.

Let me give you some direction on the process of finding an excellent real estate agent, rather than choosing the agent whose name and picture were on a sign that you passed on a random street. (Believe it or not, some people actually do this!)

EIGHT WAYS TO LOCATE A STELLAR AGENT

1. **Ask a friend or relative** who has recently moved. If they had a good experience, chances are they will gladly recommend their agent; if not, keep looking. Ask your friend what they liked or did not like about the agent, if they are willing to tell you.

2. **Look through websites** for agents who have a lot of MLS listings. This could mean they're busy, and a busy agent is usually a good agent! By the way, MLS stands for Multiple Listing Service. This is the online hub where realtors market properties for sale.

3. **Find a neighborhood specialist.** A specialist is someone who specializes in the communities where you want to buy your home. Even if an agent can represent you from another county, chances are that the agent who lives in the local market and *sells* in the local market will be more familiar with the specifications of the properties that are bought and sold within that district.

4. **Attend networking events, mixers, and lunch meetings** held by the chamber of commerce, which often have real estate agents in attendance. The fact that they took the time to be there indicates an agent who is a go-getter and who will be active in trying to find you the right property.

5. **Ask the broker of record** at a real estate agency for their best pick. A broker of record is essentially the supervisor. Call and tell them you want their star player—ideally, a seasoned, stellar agent who is patient and has great follow-through. No one knows their agents' performance better than the broker of record.

6. **Conduct interviews with agents in your area**. Then, request references and call them just the same as you would if you were interviewing a potential employee.

7. **Visit an open house** at a home that interests you. Many great agents will arrange to show a home on behalf of the homeowner, but it gives new buyers a chance to meet quality agents who can also locate properties that are similar to the prospect's requirements. Just make sure you ask up front if they're a "dual disclosed agent" or if they could represent you as a "buyer's agent" (more on this later in this chapter). This becomes important if you decide to make an offer on the same house they are showcasing.

8. **Call the local real estate board** to find out if there have been any complaints against or infractions on the agent you are considering. The board may even be able to recommend you to some of the most respected agents in the area.

Most licensed real estate agents are honorable, ethical and worth their weight in gold, but just as in every occupation, you have professionals who work at different performance levels: outstanding, good, average, or just plain bad. Poor performance can usually be attributed to a couple of factors, such as inexperience, lack of ambition or understanding of their customers' needs, or simply lack of common sense to get the job done properly.

> **CHILL PILL #4**
>
> As a rule of thumb, any well-respected agent will have plenty of references, a prominent website, a lot of listings, and a good rapport with other agents and brokers. Many people don't realize that even if a property of interest to you is listed with another agent, your own personal real estate agent can also show it to you. So no need to flip-flop with agents.

Both good and bad agents have one thing in common—their job is to be a "deal-maker." Some real estate agents will perform all sorts of tricks to "stitch up" a deal. This is fine, so long as they are not "stitching up" the buyer or the seller. There's nothing wrong with displaying enthusiasm to pull a deal together. In fact, this should be applauded. However, your agent needs to remain professional and ethical at all times throughout the process, from contract to closing.

Unfortunately, most homeowners are reasonably inexperienced when it comes to buying or selling a property. They rely greatly on the perceived abilities of the agent they are dealing with. Many homeowners are "fair game" for an inexperienced, disloyal, or dishonest agent!

In any negotiation, win–win deals are the best. Unfortunately, when buying or selling a house, things sometimes happen to benefit just one party . . . the buyer, the seller, or possibly just the real estate agent. Therein lies the danger. Who is the real estate agent really working for? Where do their true loyalties lie? With the seller, the buyer, or themselves? And how is one to know the difference before it is too late?

It's important to understand that a real estate agent can be working as a buyer's agent, a seller's agent, or a dual disclosed agent. Let's go over what these mean:

- **Buyer's Agent:** An agent whose fiduciary responsibility is with the buyer. They work solely with the buyer to represent their best interests in a real estate transaction.

- **Seller's Agent:** An agent whose fiduciary responsibility is with the seller. They work solely with the seller to represent their best interests in a real estate transaction. A seller's agent is the same as a "listing agent." The two terms are used interchangeably.

- **Dual Disclosed Agent:** An agent who represents both the buyer and seller in a real estate transaction. They must disclose their role to both and have written permission from both parties to proceed.

Dual disclosed agency can be very helpful and efficient if you are dealing with an ethical agent. It means that you have one agent overseeing the deal, so it's in their best interest to ensure that all goes well and that the deal closes. It's a win-win for the agent, because it means they'll get to keep both sides of the commission. Normally the buyer's and seller's agents split the sales commission at closing, but if one agent represents both parties, they get to keep the entire commission.

Herein also lies the trouble, because keeping the whole commission is an enticing proposition for any agent. It can also be a trick-bag for the clients of an unethical agent.

I remember a scandalous transaction that took place a few years ago: A lovely couple had narrowed down their prospects to two homes they really loved. One house was being listed by their agent, which meant he was acting as a dual agent on that one, and the house they were really leaning toward was being represented by Agent X. Ultimately the couple placed an offer on Agent X's property. Twenty-four hours later the couple received the very unpleasant news that someone else beat them to it, and the seller had taken the offer. Disappointed, the couple then placed an offer on their second choice, the property their agent listed. Well, lo and behold, eleven days before closing, the husband decided to surf the internet just to look at more homes.

Wouldn't you know it: The home they were initially in love with was still listed for sale. Confused, the husband called their agent, but got voicemail. Then he noticed the listing agent's number on a photo next to the house, so he called and inquired about the property. He was dumbstruck to find out that not only was the property still for sale, but it was also listed with a price reduction. His agent had never presented his offer. Unbelievable! They took the matter up with the agent's managing broker and with the local Real Estate Commission—and rightfully so. Ultimately, the crooked agent lost his license to sell real estate.

Again, this type of activity is *not the norm*, but it does happen. Just don't let it happen to you. Nine times out of ten there is nothing wrong with a "dual disclosed agent" relationship so long as your agent remains ethical and you feel assured that they will work in your best interest.

If you ever feel that your setup has taken a sticky turn, simply go to your agent's managing broker and request that they assign another agent to represent your side of the deal. If you do it this way, your agent shouldn't get too wrinkled about it; at least they still get to keep some of the commission as a referral.

HOW STICKING WITH ONE AGENT WORKS IN YOUR FAVOR

This brings me to the many reasons why you should stick with your real estate agent after you have found the right one.

So you want me to be loyal to you, but you're clearly noncommittal, eh? Sounds like you're talking to a new love prospect, right? Or maybe an ex? Whenever you are in a relationship, whether romantic or professional, a connection has been made. The relationship that exists between homebuyers and their real estate agents is no different than the relationship you would forge with your minister, accountant, or barber. You get to know each other and even care about each other. Many of my clients become people I care about a great deal, and I truly enjoy making their dreams of homeownership come true. Sometimes I get to work with them again a few years down the road and see their children get taller. And I have to say that these clients are people I really go the extra mile to help.

Oftentimes, homebuyers are reluctant to sign paperwork binding them to anything. Some of them would rather "test the waters" and "sow their oats," rather than settle down and "put a ring on it" by committing to a real estate agent. Unfortunately, this can present problems for homebuyers and create messy situations for all parties involved.

Why? Well, when a buyer selects one licensed real estate agent to represent them in the process of buying a home, that agent accepts what is called a "fiduciary responsibility" to that particular buyer.

According to the National Association of Realtors (NAR), the six fiduciary duties of a realtor to his or her client are loyalty, obedience, disclosure, confidentiality, reasonable care and diligence, and accounting.

Obedience means obeying the instructions of the client; reasonable care and diligence means using your skills as a real estate professional to the best of your abilities; and accounting means accurate financial record keeping. The fiduciary duties of loyalty, disclosure, and confidentiality can be a bit more complex.

Let me break them down for you:
Loyalty. This refers to the manner in which a realtor must act at all times to serve the best interests of the client,

excluding all other interests. (i.e. the realtor's own self-interests). This includes avoiding any conflicts of interest that might compromise a realtor's loyalty to her client.

Disclosure. The realtor must disclose any and all relevant information to the main client, whether they are a buyer's agent or a seller's agent. According to the NAR, if an agent represents the buyer, they must disclose:

- Any knowledge of whether a seller is likely to settle for a lower price
- Any information regarding a seller's need to sell a property
- Any legal or other relationship with a seller or a property for sale
- Any information regarding the value of a property
- The duration a property has been for sale
- A complete history of offers and counteroffers
- Any other information potentially impacting a buyer's ability to buy a property at the lowest price and with the best terms

Confidentiality. A realtor must keep the client's confidence and secrets, much the same as a doctor or someone in the legal profession. This is especially true of any information that could compromise the client's bargaining position. The responsibility to maintain confidentiality means that a real estate agent representing a seller cannot disclose to a potential buyer that the seller needs to sell the property urgently or will likely sell a property at a lower price. The agent would then be violating the "covenant of trust." On the flip side, a buyer's agent cannot disclose to a seller that the buyer will pay a higher price than the current offer.

Whew, that was a lot of information! But it's probably clear at this point that working with multiple agents instead of designating one agent is *not* in the buyer's best interest. For one thing, it can lead to confusion—who, exactly, is loyal to whom? For another, if the buyer works with just one agent, that agent is obligated to keep their best interests in mind as they work together. It's a mutually beneficial relationship.

Working with more than one agent can also be a turn-off to a seller and their real estate agent because it sends a red flag to the seller's side that this buyer could be troublesome to deal with. Not to mention, it could potentially cause a legal dispute after closing. Determining which broker from the buyer's side is entitled to earn a real estate commission check may not be clear; it may lead to disputes and hassles that cause time delays.

In contrast, working exclusively with one agent:

- **Gives homebuyers the opportunity to build a strong rapport** with an agent who can invest time in serving their needs during the buying process. And it connects buyers with a "go-to" guy or gal who has your back when it comes to buying a home, without having to worry whether the realtor is primarily serving yours or the seller's needs. In other words, it takes away the question of motives.

- **Helps to prevent buyers from missing out** on the chance of finding, bidding on, and buying the home of their dreams.

- **Gives you someone to ask for advice** on other aspects of the homebuying process, especially if you are a first-time homebuyer or just new to the process.

- **Enables you to waste less time** by having an agent work for you instead of trying to do all of the scouting, negotiating, and paperwork on your own.

Have faith in your real estate agent! If you've chosen someone with the qualities I mentioned above, then you're most likely in good hands. It is okay if you are not satisfied and want to find someone else, but just be courteous enough to make the most respectable exit as possible.

To serve as an example, I once represented a newlywed couple that had saved up money for a down payment for a couple of years toward the purchase of their first home. David and Elise were smart people with great careers in media. Overall, they seemed like nice people who appeared to have their priorities in order.

The couple had completed many of the "right" things in preparing to purchase their first home. They even attended a regional first-time homebuyer's seminar at their local community center and eventually met with two local mortgage loan officers to compare interest rates and determine how much they could afford to borrow. They asked family members who were homeowners for advice, and this is precisely where things got tricky. Prior to meeting me, David and Elise had viewed a couple of homes they liked, but both times they had made an offer, someone else beat them to the punch and they were outbid by other buyers.

Despite being advised at the seminar to meet with at least two real estate agents and choose only one that was a good fit for them to work with exclusively, this couple did the very opposite. Instead, they spent their weekends driving around through various neighborhoods of interest, hoping to find their "dream starter house."

Feeling discouraged by the results and with the home-buying process as a whole, they decided to take a different and more aggressive approach. Upon the encouragement of unwitting relatives, they planned to contact the listing agent directly and develop a rapport. The theory was that by working directly with the listing agent, it would pretty much guarantee that the sellers would accept their offer. This is a big misconception that many people have about the home-buying process. Just as in life, nothing in realty is guaranteed.

As luck would have it, after searching for an exhausting nine months and hopping from agent to agent with no luck, the couple was introduced to me. We instantly clicked, and after determining what their home-buying needs were, I found them a home they really liked.

It was a charming, three-bedroom Cape Cod situated on a nice quarter-acre plot. It had a ton of potential, but needed some sprucing up. It piqued their interest because of its proximity to a nearby beach town that they enjoyed going to as well as the convenience of public transportation into Manhattan and affordable property taxes. However, the lack of upgrades was a bit of a downer for them, so after seeing it a second time, they decided to keep searching.

A month later, I got word that some updates were done to the home. But unfortunately I was out of town and returning in two days. It was the only weekend I took off the whole month! So I called David and Elise and asked them to drive by and take a look at the new exterior. I offered to schedule an appointment for them to view it on the day I returned if they were interested. The exterior was almost unrecognizable compared to what they'd seen before. The homeowner had installed a new stucco facade, new windows, a new fence, and lush new landscaping.

The listing agent happened to be hosting an open house that day, so it gave David and Elise a chance to go inside again for the third time, without scheduling an appointment to view it. Again, they were not accompanied by the agent they had been working with for the past few months . . . Namely, ME.

Upon entering the home, they were greeted with and asked to fill out their contact info on the sign-in sheet. One of the questions asked on the questionnaire was whether they were working with an agent and, if so, to please state the agent's name and contact info. Instead of following the instructions, the newlyweds checked the box that read *"not currently represented by an agent."*

The listing agent eagerly showed them around the home. David and Elise called her that very same night and made an offer.

The agent reminded the pair that by working with her directly to purchase the home, she would be taking on the role of a "disclosed dual agent." Again, a "dual disclosed agent" is someone who works with both the buyer and the seller in a neutral fashion with no allegiance to one side or another. In many states, "dual agency" is perfectly legal and works fine between both sides of a real estate transaction. But it doesn't guarantee the best results for either buyer or seller.

The morning after the offer was made, I happened to call Elise to see if she and David had taken a look at the exterior upgrades. I also wanted to confirm our appointment to re-tour the home. I did not hear back from her. I tried again during her lunch break the next day, not knowing they had placed an offer. This time, she picked up.

Needless to say, the conversation took a turn when Elise informed me that she and David had already written an offer on the house the day before, without informing me. I felt like I had been hit with a sledgehammer! I was stunned, upset, and totally confused by their actions. I had held them in such high regard, and thought we had established an excellent rapport. At that point, I asked Elise to set up a conference call with her husband so that we could all be on the same page.

Much to my surprise and disappointment, David became very dismissive and essentially blew off the fact that I had introduced them to the house, arranged two showings, and notified them of the upgrades. I explained that the way they went about things wasn't the proper way to buy a house. I wasn't looking to hold any grudges against them. They were very inexperienced as homebuyers, so I chalked it up to their rookie status.

When I suggested that we resolve the matter ethically, the husband countered that he had no obligation to disclose our pre-existing relationship with the seller's agent. I certainly couldn't twist his arm or force him to do what was right, but I did have a signed buyer's agency agreement, and an ethical obligation to disclose our pre-existing relationship to the listing agent. The way things work in the real estate business is that the agent who is the "procuring cause" of a client being introduced to a home is the one entitled to the commission, or in some cases partial commission.

CHILL PILL #5

Unless your agent has done something truly horrible or unethical, it is considered unacceptable and in poor taste to exclude them from participating in the offer you make on a property they found on your behalf.

So I called the seller's agent to let her know that I had shown them the home twice before the upgrades were completed. I didn't want to get in the middle of a dispute, but frankly, if I hadn't shared this information with the listing agent, we could have all potentially wound up in court over something that was clearly avoidable. The real estate business is a close-knit community, and dishonesty always comes back to bite you.

Soon after our conversation, the agent called David and Elise to tell them that the sellers had accepted another offer that had been submitted by a different agent. In this case, perhaps the buyers' dishonesty—intentional or not—had something to do with the fact that their offer was not accepted by the sellers. In any case, they didn't end up with the home of their dreams.

The lesson here is this: When you exclude someone who has been working diligently for you and spending their time and resources to help you, it is dishonest to leave that person out of the transaction. Not only could this result in ill feelings or an undesirable outcome, as with the newlyweds, but it could also result in a lawsuit or legal hassles.

As the saying goes, *"Honesty is always the best policy!"* It's true for both sides.

CHAPTER 3

DON'T WORRY, BUY HAPPY!

Finding the Home of Your Dreams

FINALLY, YOU'RE READY TO START LOOKING. THIS will probably be your favorite part of the home-buying process. Getting into a house and walking the floor plan, backyard, and neighborhood is not only fun, but it can also help you make the best decision on which home feels like the best fit for your family's needs.

After seeing a handful of homes, you may find that you are overwhelmed by the details. It's very common to see three or four homes and by the next day have a hard time remembering which house was which. Did house number two have the landscaped backyard or did house number three? Did house number one have the oak cabinetry? Or was it the second house? Trust me: I've seen it happen time and time again.

To avoid confusion, here are a few quick tips to aid you in an organized and progressive search:

Never see more than five homes in a day. You will be mentally exhausted trying to remember the details of each. Additionally, you should take your time in each home to fully examine what it has to offer.

Keep a log. I always recommend keeping track of the homes you've seen in a small notebook. Take notes about your likes and dislikes. Or put together a spreadsheet where you can compare each home's features and amenities. Some items to note would be:

- Does the home layout work for your family's needs?
- Size of kitchen
- Number of bedrooms and bathrooms and their dimensions
- Square footage of the house
- Storage space, including closets and cupboards
- Does it include a basement (finished or unfinished)? Does it include a garage?
- Landscaping condition
- Size of yard and/or privacy of backyard
- Paint condition, including ceiling spackle

- Chips or cracks in flooring or tile
- Are the windows and doors sound? How new are they?
- Is the foundation sound? Are the walls free of cracks and visible repairs?
- When was the last time the roof tiles or shingles were replaced?
- How new are the appliances? Were records kept?
- How new is the heating or AC unit? Does the home have ceiling fans?
- Is it well insulated and ventilated?
- How old are the electrical wires?
- Is it close to any major disturbances—train tracks, highways, schools, etc.?
- Is the neighborhood safe?
- What type of conveniences are nearby—stores, shopping plazas, restaurants, post office, banks, etc.?
- Age of home
- History of property ownership

Take photos. Normally, your agent will send you an MLS listing of the property. But in case the listing doesn't include a substantial number of photos, take a camera or a camera phone with you.

Narrow down your top three. After seeing a handful of homes, start narrowing down your prospects. Revisit all of your top picks. At second glance you may notice something you didn't see the first-time around.

Visit your prospective home at different times of day.
Homes may appear different during the day than they do
at night. It is also wise to visit the home again right after
a heavy rain if you can manage it. Homeowners can mask
water damage when the weather is dry. But chances are,
when it's raining or has rained recently, the house will tell on
itself. Go straight to the basement and notice the smell. Does
it smell or feel damp? If so, water may be getting in.

THE TRICK TO CUTTING
THE FAT IN YOUR HOME SEARCH

As I mentioned in the chapter about choosing an agent, if you
find a very competent and experienced realtor, then your search
should not take long. He or she can narrow down your criteria
with very little effort and can also give you the best advice as to
which properties offer the best value to you as a homebuyer.

According to national statistics, the average buyer sees twelve
homes before making a purchase. Of course, there are those who
see more and those who see less. Every now and again I run into
buyers who want to see everything on the market before making
a decision. I mean literally *everything*. Please don't be that kind of
buyer. Nothing will make an agent run away from you faster than
acting like a kid in a candy store.

In my entire real estate career, I've only had to fire one client.
Yes, real estate agents can fire you as well! Jessie was a thirty-four

year old bachelorette from Bergen County, New Jersey. She had an ideal profile as a homebuyer. Her credit score was 780; she'd been at her job for more than six years, and she had a sizable down payment. There were no immediate red flags.

I asked her to come up with a wish list, which is something I do with each of my clients to help them narrow down their choices. Jessie wanted a three-bedroom townhome in a swimming-pool community with low HOA fees, new appliances, and new or updated features throughout. She preferred move-in ready, but she absolutely did not want to live within a few block's radius of a school because of the noise. So far so good, right?

On the first day of our home tour I explained to Jessie that we would be seeing five homes per day so that she could retain the information. She was appalled and demanded to see more. Her reasoning was that she got very little time off of work and needed to make the most of it. To accommodate her request, I suggested we fit in one or two more, which was against my better judgment. Her response was that she'd be happier with seeing ten or twelve that day. How absurd! As a thorough agent, I make it my business to preview all homes that my clients visit so that I can ensure their time is not wasted. This also helps to narrow down the homes they need to see before making an offer. It saves everyone time and energy. Ten to twelve was just not necessary in one day.

After a week of home searching, Jessie came to my office without a scheduled appointment with a handful of listings she found online and wanted to see that day. Many of them were far out of her price range and search criteria. I explained to her that I had three other clients that day, but could preview some of the houses by the next day and show her a few. The next day, I sorted out five of the twenty-five homes she brought me based on those that suited her wish list. My client was visibly angry that she could not see all of them that day. I explained to her that she requested a three bedroom townhome, and some of the listings were for five bedroom single family homes that were almost $100,000 over her budget. She also mentioned that she didn't want to live near schools because of the noise. Well, two of the homes were on the same block as a firehouse and one was literally across the park from an elementary school. She even included condominiums in buildings with HOA fees that were over $1,200 per month. It was the complete opposite of everything she said she wanted. Confused, I asked if she was changing her mind on her initial wish list, and her answer was, "No, I still really want a townhouse." I advised her that most of the listings she requested to see were far out of her search criteria and budget. Her response? "That may be true, but I still want to at least see them." Clearly she wasn't getting the concept of a wish list or search criteria.

After two months of working with Jessie, I decided to gracefully bow out. Her search could have lasted more than a year and probably did. She wasn't being fair or realistic to me, or to herself. It was a lose-lose situation.

When discussing your needs with your agent, be detailed. The more information they are armed with, the more they can help you. At the very beginning of your search, write down *everything* you absolutely want in your home, *everything* you absolutely don't want, and a list of things you are willing to compromise on. If you are searching with a partner, it's important that you do this both individually and also together.

Here are some things to think about when creating your wish list:

- **Style of home:** Single-family, townhouse, condo?

- **Price range:** What is your comfort zone? What's the absolute highest you can go for a home you love?

- **Taxes**: What's the most you want to pay?

- **Location:** Where are your top three areas to live?

- **Distance:** How far to work, friends, family?

- **Amenities:** Swimming, tennis, clubhouse, gated?

- **Square footage:** How large or small?

- **Number of beds and baths:** Three or four? More?

- **Flooring:** Hardwood, carpet, tile?

- **Age of home:** Newer or older?

- **Condition:** Move-in ready or in need ofupdates?

- **Parking:** Driveway, garage, or carport?

- **Outdoor space:** Backyard, fenced-in, deck, garden?

- **Neighborhood:** Near schools, shopping, residential, urban? What about diversity? Or lack of diversity?

Once you've crafted your wish list, the key is to stick to it! This ensures you'll have a successful search and be happy with your purchase in the end. Now, we do have an offbeat saying in our field that *"buyers are liars."* LOLOL! This is often because buyers tend to start out adamant about what is "non-negotiable" for them. But by the end of the process they've eventually done a complete one-eighty. My clients and I often laugh about this exact thing when we get to the closing table.

It's okay if your needs or wish list change in the process of your search. It's wise to reevaluate the list if you have veered too far away from your definite needs or your bottom-line budget.

CHILL PILL #6

If your needs change, be sure to communicate your new criteria to your agent immediately so they can be more effective in helping you.

WHY YOU SHOULD
LOOK UNDER THE HOOD
BEFORE MAKING AN OFFER

You wouldn't buy a used car without looking under the hood, so why would you buy a home without checking it over thoroughly? Find out as much as possible about the history of the home. How many owners have lived in it? Was it a rental or owner-occupied prior to being put on the market? When were the latest renovations made? What types of home improvements have been made? How recently were they done?

Every home has a backstory. Normally the MLS (Multiple Listing System) offers limited information about the home. Depending on the MLS system (they vary from state to state), you can usually find the price paid by the current homeowner, when they bought it, and any price reductions. To get accurate and up-to-date information about property taxes, you'll need to research the county tax records. To learn whether there were ever any fires or floods, you may want to pay a visit to the local fire department or to the county clerk's office. This information is available to you with very little digging—most of it can be found on the Internet. A great agent will research this for you without having to be asked. But making sure this is being done may behoove you! It's much the same as requesting a "Carfax" report on a used vehicle. You don't want to get stuck with a lemon.

Next, evaluate other considerations, like the neighborhood and even the neighbors who live on each side of you. While this may not be a deal breaker, it's important to know if you will like living there. You are buying more than just the house. You are buying the neighborhood and everyone in it.

Take a walk around the block. Do families live in the neighborhood? Mostly old or young? Single or with children? Are there any dangerous dogs? Do you feel like you have anything in common with the neighbors? Do they seem welcoming and friendly, or disinterested? Does this even matter to you?

If you have children, consider the school district. If public schools rank low in that particular area, do you have other options available, such as private schools? This factor can affect resale.

Is the community in support of the neighborhood's rebirth and development? Finding a home in an up-and-coming neighborhood could mean that your home will increase in value over the next five to ten years, but buying a home in a declining market could leave you upside down if you ever want to sell. You can find out about any short- and long-term development by contacting the community planning and development department for the municipality. Every town has a department such as this. They are responsible for coordinating the long-range planning for each town.

In my opinion, location is *the* most important thing you should be mindful of when shopping for real estate. I've seen it happen dozens of times: A client falls head over heels in love with a house without fully considering the neighborhood. They buy the house, move in . . . and then they meet the crazy neighbors. Think about it. If you have a nice house in a crummy neighborhood, then you may not be happy and could even be risking your safety. Most people do their grocery shopping, participate in lifestyle events, and run errands within a mile of their home. So it's important that you feel comfortable within your chosen community.

> ### CHILL PILL #7
>
> If you feel strongly about a home you have previewed, go back and visit it again prior to making an offer. You may see things that you missed in the first tour, especially if you have visited a number of properties.

Don't forget the example of the Natasha, the Boston buyer, whom I mentioned in the introduction. Those railroad tracks can be misleading! Had Natasha done her homework, she would have known that the train ran by at least two or three times each hour, rather than two or three times per day. That's a big difference!

So take time and do your homework. Observe the surrounding landscape. Is there anything loud or undesirable nearby? Are there any factories, loud highways, or high-traffic scenarios? For instance, people who live near schools may be detained for a couple of hours every afternoon while waiting for the kids to be picked up or bussed home. Is there anything about the community that you don't like, but that may end up being a small sacrifice because you like everything else?

Location is critical, friends! Quality of life is the reason to buy in the first place, so make sure you choose something that is comfortable and inviting. Of course, you can't control future circumstances like having a neighbor move in next door who has the world's largest hubcap collection. For now, if everything looks great, then you have to assess whether the quality of life is in line with your individual preferences, likes, lifestyle, and comfort zone.

SMART TIPS FOR BUYING IN AN HOA OR GATED COMMUNITY

In many states across the country, you will find an abbreviation next to certain homes listed on the MLS that says, "HOA Community," particularly in subdivisions, gated communities or in clusters of townhomes. What does this mean?

HOA stands for Homeowners Association, which is an organization that oversees the properties within a particular development, district, or specific area in which the home is located. Sometimes there are less than a hundred of these homes in one neighborhood, while other times you will find hundreds of homes within a development or area.

The job of the HOA is to oversee and enforce the rules of the community and maintain the integrity of the homes within it. In some communities the HOA covers all of the landscaping services, garbage pickup, and maintainance of common areas like the pool or clubhouse.

In HOA communities there are often guidelines to follow when keeping pets on a leash or picking up after them. I don't know about you, but I find it offensive when a neighbor lets their pooch lay down a fresh one on my sidewalk! This rarely happens in a community with an HOA.

The HOA typically collects a fee from members, so if you happen to buy a home within one of these communities you will have additional monthly or yearly dues to pay on top of your monthly mortgage payment. Make sure you factor this in, just the same as you would put your utility bills or car payment within your monthly budget.

On the "pro" side of living in an HOA community (which can be either gated or not gated, by the way), you will most likely have more amenities and conveniences. For example, a lot of communities have a fitness center, pool, banquet facilities for you to host a party, and the landscaping will be beautifully managed for you without having to spend money on a landscaper. This can be a good way to look at the extra expense of the HOA dues in that you may end up saving money on something else.

Other communities have bike paths, gyms for volleyball or racquetball games, billiards tables, and car ports or individual garages for members. Every community is different, so the amenities that you will find will vary from one place to the next . . . but so do the rules!

The rules can sometimes be a turnoff, especially for those people who are used to having flexibility. If you like to park your boat or your '66 Corvette with a cover in your driveway for an extended period of time, then a home in an HOA community is probably not for you.

HOA communities can be strict. If you leave your garbage can out for an extra day because you forgot to carry it back from the curb, you might be at risk of getting a warning or even a fine from the HOA. These are some of the drawbacks that you should be aware of.

Another complaint of residents is that HOAs are less "people-oriented" and are all business; they may be less responsive to a homeowner's needs. If you have a complaint to take up with the HOA or you want an exception to the rules, the association may need to have a special meeting. You could end up having to wait a long time for your concern to be taken care of. This totally depends on the size and responsiveness of the HOA, two factors you should investigate prior to actually purchasing a home.

CHILL PILL #8

Before you buy in a community with an HOA, get a "bylaw" book and read every rule listed to see if the property is going to be a good fit for your desires, needs, and the freedoms you currently enjoy. You may like the extra attention and community atmosphere of living in an HOA community, or you may find the rules too rigid for your taste.

Keep in mind that the HOA might need to "approve" you as a resident or tenant of that community. Their job is to keep the neighborhood safe, so if you like to participate in any questionable activities or do things that are outside of the "norm," a community with an HOA may not be a good fit for you.

For instance, I know a guy who bought a townhouse in an HOA community and was told that each property owner was required to give the HOA access to each residence in the community once every six months for a smoke detector test. Their rationale was that if one of the townhomes caught fire, then all of the houses on that block would also be at risk. Even though this seemed like a pretty reasonable rule, he was the "rebellious" type who refused to abide by the rules and let the HOA come into his home.

Eventually, the HOA took the homeowner to court. It cost him a lot of money to hire a lawyer, and he lost the case. It was clearly written in the bylaws before he bought the house. Even though it was his home, he was out of line and not compliant. After losing and spending a lot of time and money in legal hassles, he was ordered by the court to allow the HOA in bi-annually for the smoke detector test. He also had to pay their legal fees in addition to his own.

Now, I want to be clear: Millions of people buy homes in HOA communities and are very happy. It is professional, usually very orderly, and safe. Despite the ground rules, there are always those few people who think that living in an HOA community is no different from any other neighborhood, and because they "own" their home, they should be allowed to do whatever they want on the grounds of their own property. This is a valid argument, and I can see both sides; therefore, I make it a point to find out what my clients expect before showing any homes in communities with an HOA.

I once had a gentleman who bought his house and then a few months later, wanted to break ground on a new swimming pool in his backyard. Unfortunately, it was against the HOA policies! Boy, he was as mad as a hornet after you pick the flower it was just about to land on! I had to remind him that he was given the HOA bylaws in advance and neglected to read them.

CONSIDER THESE SEVEN THINGS WHEN CONSIDERING A HOME IN AN HOA COMMUNITY:

1. **Fees:** How much are the fees for the residents? They could be anywhere between $50 and $1,000 or more per month, depending on the affluence of the neighborhood, how many other homes share the HOA dues (distribution of fees), and what those fees generally cover. Most often, they include the maintenance of all common areas, including property landscaping, the clubhouse, playground, and pool.

2. **Rules:** Are the covenants (bylaws) too strict for your taste? Or are they something you can live with? For example, in some HOA divisions there may be rules about what color your house must be, right down to the shutter colors, railing, and front door. There may be rules about what you can park in your own driveway or even what window treatments you can use.

3. **Quality of Management:** There are HOAs that are known to be too strict and over-managed, where the least infraction can cost you a hefty fine. Then there are those that are under-managed, where no one seems to give a hoot about the cracks in the sidewalks or shingles falling off the roofs, leaving properties looking less than desirable.

4. **Pet Policies:** Be aware that some dog breeds may be restricted (particularly larger or more aggressive breeds). Other rules regarding pets often apply, especially regarding poop pickup duties, dog bites, and leaving a dog outside. Even if you *don't* have a pet, read this rule just in case one day you change your mind and want to know the rules about what you can and can't do.

5. **Impact on Your Monthly Budget:** Do the extra HOA dues put your mortgage calculations over budget? If you have to adjust to accommodate HOA fees, then your new house could become a financial disaster.

6. **Drama:** Dig a little deeper into the "feeling" of the community. Ask your realtor to get a copy of the last HOA meeting transcript to find out any past or current conflicts that exist between members of the community. The last thing you want to do is put yourself in the midst of drama! You can find out if any lawsuits exist or if only certain neighbors have complained. If you're lucky, this will be a peaceful community that is well managed.

7. **Past problems:** Is the home you want to buy currently in compliance with the HOA? The last thing you want to do is take over someone else's previous headache, so see if you can get a home history and determine whether any prior issues exist.

Under no circumstance do I wish to deter you from buying in an HOA community if that is the right choice for you and your family. However, if you are someone who dislikes rules or who doesn't like to be told what to do, then perhaps your personality might not be the best fit and you should consider buying elsewhere.

CHAPTER 4

DISTRESSED PROPERTIES:
Are They Really Worth the Hunt?

AS A GENERAL PIECE OF ADVICE, I WOULD SAY THAT you should stick to finding a home the traditional way if this is your first-time. You're likely to have a more pleasant experience than going the route of purchasing a distressed property. However, this doesn't mean that if a good short sale or foreclosure opportunity comes your way, you shouldn't attempt to pursue it. I just want to make sure you are informed about the extra complications you may have to handle.

In case you are wondering what it means for a property to be distressed, let's explore this bit of real estate lingo. A "distressed" property refers to a house that must be sold because of the previous owner's inability to pay their mortgage. Depending on how cooperative the owner is, sometimes the bank tries to work things out with them, but if negotiations fail, it leaves only a few possibilities.

- **Short Sale:** This is a sale in which the proceeds from selling the property will fall short of what is still owed on the property. This includes liens against the property—that is, legal claims that must be paid before the property is sold. In a short sale, the lien holders agree to let the lien go and accept less than the amount owed, so the house might be listed for much less than it is worth. This is better than foreclosure, because it results in fewer fees and costs, but in both foreclosures and short sales, the homeowner ends up with a negative credit report.

- **Foreclosure**: Simply put, foreclosure is the process by which a homeowner's right to a property is forfeited because of failure to pay the mortgage. If the owner cannot pay off the outstanding debt or sell it via short sale, the property then goes to a foreclosure auction where potential buyers can bid on the property.

- **REO Property or Real Estate Owned**: When the house still goes unpurchased either by an investor or through a foreclosure auction, the bank will then list the house for sale with a seller's agent. At this point the bank is very motivated to sell the home!

With any distressed real estate property, be forewarned that there may be more complications than with a house that is being sold for other reasons. It is better not to get emotionally attached to any property you find in foreclosure or at auction.

A perfect story that comes to mind is of clients who came to me after trying their hand at foreclosure auctions. An adorable older couple, Josef and Hanna, originally came from Poland. They were self-made, having successfully run a family business in the United States for almost twenty years.

As Hanna explained, they had attended a few seminars on "real estate investing" and "tricks to successfully buying foreclosures." When they embarked on their new home search, Josef was adamant that it had to be a foreclosure. And he was confident that he knew all there was to know about the process after attending these seminars and reading a few books.

To make a long story short, by the time they threw in the towel and came to me, they'd been to nineteen foreclosure auctions and lost out on all eleven homes they bid on.

What they had not anticipated was the amount of research and work they'd need to put into the process to ensure they were making a sound investment. Week after week, Josef would go to the courthouse and get the list of new foreclosures. After work, he and Hanna would drive around to all of the homes on the list to view the exteriors. On a few occasions, they found themselves face-to-face with disgruntled homeowners who were irate the bank was foreclosing! At the auctions, they nervously bid on properties without inspection or even getting a chance to see the interior, other than a few old photos they found online.

The most defeating part of the process for Josef was that after all of his research and hard work, and after taking valuable hours off from his business to attend the auctions, he'd walk away empty-handed. Having been outbid by investors time and time again, and beat out by cash-on-site deals, he decided it was no longer worth his time or trouble.

Ultimately, I found Hanna and Josef a terrific five-bedroom home in superb condition. The kicker was that the sellers needed to sell quickly because they were relocating. So they accepted the offer for $23,000 lower than what it appraised for. In the end, Josef declared, "We wasted our time for months trying to score a foreclosure. My time alone was worth more than what I would have saved if we had gotten one."

CHILL PILL #9

Shopping exclusively for a foreclosure is not something I recommend. If things work out that way, great! But don't be narrow-sighted about it, because you could miss out on an opportunity to buy an undervalued home in a great neighborhood. Motivated sellers can often run you an even better deal than a distressed property.

THE REAL DEAL WITH
SHORT SALES & FORECLOSURES

Many people set their minds on buying a foreclosure simply because they've heard rumors about steals on price. They erroneously believe they will get a better deal than if they purchase a home on the regular market.

Historically, foreclosures have been equitable for skilled buyers. The trouble is that the foreclosure secret is no longer a secret, and in many cities, there is a lot of competition when bidding at auctions for the small inventory of worthwhile foreclosures out there. I'm sure you don't need me to illustrate for you what happens when bidding starts to heat up, do you? That's right; it drives the price up, many times to market value. So is it really that good of a deal in the end?

Buying distressed property is not for everyone, and there are many factors to consider when buying a foreclosure. For example, when a bank takes over a property from a homeowner in default, the house is often in need of major repairs. The homeowner has been in financial crisis and perhaps unable to stay on top of maintenance. The need for roof repairs, old appliances, floor and ceiling replacements, and even electrical rewiring are not uncommon in foreclosures and bank takeovers.

Some homeowners even deliberately ruin the home or in some cases, have moved away from the area with nobody there to maintain it. This can lead to other problems, such as unwanted critters, vandalism, missing fixtures, and other strange and unforeseen problems.

In many cases, you may not even get to see the inside of a fore-closed property. If the owners still inhabit the place or if the bank is located in another state or the home is tied up in legal matters, this makes presenting the house to the general public for viewing very difficult.

The other challenge with foreclosures is that there may be liens on the property due to the owner's failure to keep up with taxes, insurance, and other matters. Therefore, the town or municipality has a right to place a lien on the house and land, which requires extra paperwork and hassle for the eventual buyer.

Another reason not to get your hopes up about buying a short sale or foreclosure is that, much like my lovely couple, you will be competing with experienced investors, many of whom have deep pockets. You may not even have a chance to compete. Many of these professional home shoppers are in a financial position to seal cash offers, which banks love when they want to unload a property. That doesn't mean the bank would snub its nose at any offer; however, your traditional 20 percent down—as well as the hassle of sorting out the mortgage paperwork—may not be as appealing to the bank as finding a buyer who is able to free them of their burden with cash.

Another complication to consider with distressed proper-ties is whether the battle between the bank and the homeowner is still pending, which could make it difficult for you to evict the occupants from the house. Some desperate homeowners rent their place out in hopes of obtaining any kind of income to pay the mortgage company and other bills. So if a third-party tenant is living in the home and has signed a lease with the homeowner, and the homeowner has defaulted on the loan, this could also be potentially nightmarish. Unfortunately, these are common scenarios.

Since the real estate bubble burst in 2007, there have been upwards of 2.2 million short sales. Many owners were upside down on their properties and decided to sell them in a short sale, meaning an approximate 10 to 20 percent discount for buyers. In 2007 and 2008, short sales seemed like an interesting prospect. The banks were short-staffed in their loss mitigation departments and overloaded with short sales. Often, they were happy just to get an offer. Since the restructuring of the banks, however, most are no longer letting go of their short sale properties at such deep discounts.

The other challenge with short sales can be hearing back from the bank in a reasonable amount of time. When buying both short sales and foreclosures, you are at the mercy of the bank. Depending on the person handling the case, the process can move at a decent pace, or it can move at a snail's pace. I've seen some short sales take up to six months, and I've seen some close in less than thirty days.

If you do find a foreclosure or short sale to buy, make sure you find out whether title problems or unpaid taxes exist that might delay your closing. These seemingly small details can add up to one giant frustration!

If you do want to proceed with a distressed property, there are a few things you need to know. First, you will have to do a lot of research and due diligence. Your real agent can help with that. The inspection, of course, is mandatory in my opinion under these circumstances, because you really need to make sure the electrical, plumbing, roof, etc., are up to livable standards. We'll talk more about the importance of a home inspection in Chapter 8.

If the inspection comes back with a list of thousands of dollars in recommended repairs, renovations, and home updates, you should consider getting some accurate and competitive quotes from reputable contractors. And if the repairs cost more than what you would save buying a home that is move-in ready, then you must truly ask yourself if buying the house is even worth it.

This also applies to tax liens. If the amount owed in back taxes is a lot higher than what you would pay for a clear title and deed, there again, this is really not the best idea for you.

Best-case scenario: you successfully find a short sale or fore-closure that is practically a steal and you need to invest very little money to fix up. Kudos to you if you find one of these gems at a great price! Though it's rarer these days, it does happen.

THE ABC'S OF REAL ESTATE SUPPLY & DEMAND, AND WHAT THEY MEAN FOR YOU

As I mentioned earlier, the real estate market goes through cycles of highs and lows. I suppose it's a lot like other industries that coincide with the economy, except that the real estate market is also one of the main predictors of the economy. Apart from

Wall Street, I don't think there is a more critical indicator that determines how analysts, economists, financial planners, and the entire business world maps the rise or decline of the economy.

One phenomenon that drives the highs and lows of the housing market—and that can affect you as a potential buyer—is a shortage in available homes. Inventory shortage is when there are more people who want to buy or rent a home than there are homes available in the marketplace. The homes that are vacant may be held off the market for a number of reasons. For example, during a time of heavy foreclosures when you would imagine there are plenty of vacant homes, it still seems impossible to find the right one at the right price. The empty homes may not be listed or available on the MLS because they need repairs or because they are tied up in legal issues, or even due to investors or banks waiting to put them up for rent or sale.

During an inventory shortage, both buyers and renters have fewer choices of available homes. This can create a spike in both purchase and rental prices. Often, an inventory shortage can make it a "sellers' market," meaning that sellers sell high and buyers have less negotiating power. Less flexibility makes it tempting to overpay, especially if you get involved in a bidding war for a home you really want and there are multiple offers on the table.

But there is a notable difference between *inventory* shortages and *housing* shortages. A housing shortage happens when there are simply not enough homes available—a major problem whenever it occurs. An inventory shortage, on the other hand, means there are plenty of vacant homes out there but they are not for sale or rent. How can the houses for sale be low in number when the vacancy rate is high? Again . . . the houses are not being presented to consumers, which in fact is a current problem at the time of this book's release. This can happen when banks or other institutions own a large number of properties and have not yet put them on the market. We've seen this happen time and time again over the past few years due to high owner default rates.

The US census is the best place to research these trends so that buyers and renters don't overpay. For example, between 2012 and the end of 2013, many homes in need of repair were being "prepped" before they were placed on the market. This could be due to the many foreclosures caused by the housing bubble of 2006 to 2007, when house prices were at an all-time high and mortgage companies were lending to underqualified homebuyers.

After the housing bubble burst, the banks became a lot more cautious in who they lent to, and it became even more difficult to get a loan for a home. As we will talk about in the upcoming chapter on financing, the banks now only lend to people who meet the right criteria and who have a substantial down payment, savings account, and steady flow of income.

Just like other trends, a real estate inventory shortage doesn't last forever. The homes that are being prepared for sale or rent will eventually become available. After these homes are added to the current inventory, it will gradually level the crazy spikes in rental prices or asking prices, and will turn it once again into a buyers' market instead of a sellers' market.

The real estate market goes up and down like a yo-yo. If you look at history, this has been going on since the beginning of the twentieth century. Depressions in the economy don't last. So, don't get depressed if you can't find the house of your dreams at the price you want to pay today! Just wait until the time is right, and I promise you that everything will fall into place naturally for you and with less effort than if you try to force it.

Sometimes I have clients who ask, "Well, if there aren't enough homes available to buy or rent, why don't they build more?"

That is a great question! The simple answer is that construction companies are typically hesitant to build new houses when there are many vacant homes sitting. Builders have suffered the crushing side effects of the housing industry bubble. It is also more difficult for new builders to emerge because of the lengths they must go through to obtain the appropriate financing, licensing, and insurance.

Do you remember not so long ago when we were reading about people who lost their entire life savings to these con artists who presented themselves as "building contractors" but were instead fly-by-night companies that did shoddy work? The industry adjusted to get rid of these supposed contractors by making it more difficult for someone to get a license and insurance as a building contractor. This was actually a game changer and a good thing for the industry because it gave the legitimate builders more staying power and credibility.

EIGHT SUREFIRE WAYS TO FIND YOUR DREAM HOME, EVEN DURING AN INVENTORY SHORTAGE

I know you love lists, so I've made this list of eight ways you can still find your dream house during an inventory shortage.

1. **Find a "Make Me Move" Listing.** What is this? Homeowners now have an option to post a price they would entertain to move from their house, without actually placing it on the market. This is a cool concept that enables a seller to post a price they would accept if you were willing to pay it, which is great if you are shopping for a house in a particular neighborhood or school district and can't seem to find anything suitable. Google "Make Me Move," and you will find this as the first listing if you want to give it a try.

2. **Ask Your Realtor About Pocket Listings.** Your real estate agent usually has access to listings that are not publicly advertised or that do not have signage. Although this is not the case with every market, in heavily populated metropolitan areas or luxury markets, there are sellers who don't want to publicly advertise and would rather sell privately. Real estate agents network with each other to find buyers for those sellers who wish to remain anonymous.

3. **Find "Pre-Market Listings" Before They Hit the MLS.** If you are working with an experienced agent and not a rookie, then most of the best real estate firms have access to forthcoming listings a few weeks ahead of time. If your agent is in the know, then he or she can beat the general public to the punch by having access to these pre-listings that can't be found elsewhere.

4. **Scour Rental Properties.** A lot of homeowners got in a bind when they overpaid for a house during the housing boom, making it tough for them to sell due to being "upside down," which means they owe more on the house than what it is actually worth. So their solution was to rent it for a few years. In other cases, the owner may have had to move away and couldn't find a buyer fast enough to make the transition to a new place. So instead of putting it up for sale, they decided to rent it for a few years. If the house is now vacant and available for rent again, it can't hurt to ask the current owner if they have any interest in selling. Or maybe they'll be interested in selling once the current renter's lease is up. Perhaps they are tired of being landlords, especially if they're managing the property from a distance. Your offer might be just the answer to their prayers!

5. **Dig for Withdrawn Listings.** When a homeowner isn't sure whether or not they want to sell or rent their home, they can be wishy-washy about posting it for sale. I have seen some homes placed on the market only to be pulled

off again a month later. If you check out the history of the property (which anyone can do on Zillow or Trulia), you can see how many times the owner has done this. Maybe nobody was offering the right price or they weren't one hundred percent sure they wanted to sell it. Ask your real estate broker to contact the owner with expressed interest in their property to see if they will entertain the idea of selling.

6. **Find Expired Listings.** If a seller's agent fails to sell a home, then the listing expires after the duration of the contract, typically after six months or one year. Perhaps other buyers thought the asking price was too high or unrealistic compared to others in the market, or maybe the homeowner just had a lazy real estate agent. It happens!

A current client of mine who is selling her home said, "My previous agent did nothing. He just stuck a sign on my lawn and that's it. I had to market the house myself because he didn't bring any prospects over and never had one single open house. I think he only showed the place twice in the entire time I hired him."

7. **Network.** Talk to people about your desire to find a place in a certain neighborhood or district. Chances are, they know somebody who has been on the fence about selling their house, and maybe the two of you can sort it out! Don't forget to bring your agent along to help you with the negotiating.

8. **Consider "For Sale by Owner" Homes (aka FSBO's).** Some rookie sellers choose to sell their home without the help of a realtor, either due to having had a bad experience with a lazy real estate agent or just being stubborn, or thinking they can do it better alone, or because they don't want to pay a commission. What they fail to realize is that by doing this, they do not have the reach or the clout that hiring an agency can offer. Nevertheless, you may just find one of these homes either by driving by and seeing a sign, or even through the previously mentioned tip of networking.

CHILL PILL #10

Enduring inventory shortage does not mean that you will be unable to find the perfect house to buy; it simply means you might have to wait longer to find it. As they say, sometimes you have to kiss a lot of frogs before you find a prince, and this applies to house shopping, too!

CHAPTER 5

THE DOWN AND DIRTY ABOUT DOWN PAYMENTS:
Knowing What You Can Afford

I T CAN BE EASY TO GET LOST IN THE IDEA OF BUYING your own house, especially if this is your first-time. You may have private daydreams of coming home, throwing off your coat, and sinking in with a good book in front of your elegant fireplace, or having the freedom to decorate as you please. Homeownership can be a joyful experience, indeed.

However, before you get too lost in those daydreams, there is one minor detail you must have thought of by now. That's right: Money.

Ah, yes. It all boils down to financial matters, doesn't it? So before you begin your quest to start shopping for the house of your dreams, there is one very fundamental task that you must take care of ahead of time.

Before you obtain a mortgage—or even a lender's green light that you can be approved for one—there is one very important thing you must have in hand, for the sake of both the lender and the seller. You've got it. It's the down payment!

Preapproval is essential, but having a down payment requires long-term planning. Those days of 100 percent financing no longer exist after the housing crash of 2007 to 2008, which still ripples through the economy in today's housing industry. Most banks feel that the homeowner should have a vested interest in the home, making them less likely to default on the mortgage.

However, you may want to look into the programs that assist first-time homebuyers. These programs vary depending on the state you live in. Some are designed to help low-income or minority families raise the money to put down for a home. Areas going through a rejuvenation often have HUD homes available. This can be a great stepping stone for first-time homebuyers.

For example, in Atlanta there is a program called the Atlanta Affordable Homeownership Program (AAHOP) as well as the Homeownership Assistance Program (HOAP). Both help buyers who are in need of down payment assistance and closing costs. These are not suited for everyone, but there are similar programs in other states that anyone considering purchasing property should look into.

The California Housing Finance Agency offers the Affordable Housing Partnership Program (AHPP) and the California

Homebuyer's Down Payment Assistance Program (CHDAP) to qualifying borrowers who are in need of a down payment and closing costs.

Who knows, maybe one of these programs is right for you and can give you the boost you need to finally start shopping for a great new home for you and your family! I strongly encourage you to look into programs offered by your state.

WHAT IS THE MAGIC NUMBER?

IN THE PROPERTY INDUSTRY, THE "MAGIC NUMBER" that lenders request you pay toward the purchase of your house is 20 percent of the purchase price. Yes, you can get an FHA loan (Federal Housing Administration) with 3.5 percent down or even find a program for 10 percent down. But 20 percent is the down payment amount that lenders have determined minimizes risk level. Therefore, if you put down 20 percent upfront, your lender sees you as someone who is less likely to default on the loan than those who have no vested interest. In other words, you are a serious-minded buyer.

A sizable investment gives you an extra incentive to meet your mortgage repayments, because if you default and lose your house, then you will have also lost a significant amount of money. Your ability to save for a 20 percent down payment also demonstrates to the mortgage lender that you are able to budget, save, and that you are fiscally responsible. These types of borrowers are more likely to carry some kind of investment or savings account, thereby assuring the likeliness of having sufficient funds available to make timely mortgage payments.

ADVANTAGES OF A 20 PERCENT DOWN PAYMENT

- Lenders perceive you as less of a risk, so they are more likely to offer you a better interest rate than those who put less money up front. As a result, you will save thousands of dollars on the reduced interest costs during the life of the loan.

- The less you need to borrow, the smaller your monthly repayments, and the less interest you will need to pay overall. Your payments will be lower, thereby making it more comfortable for you and your family to enjoy life, rather than being "house poor."

- Additionally, with a 20 percent down payment, many lenders won't require you to purchase private mortgage insurance (PMI), which protects the lender against non-payment should you default on your loan.

- The 20 percent down payment represents the equity in your home. At a later stage, you can borrow against this equity if you want to remodel or for other reasons.

CAN YOU BUY WITH A 10 PERCENT DOWN PAYMENT?

Depending on the cost of your home, a 20 percent down payment can represent a large amount of money. Many homebuyers have difficulty saving up for a large down payment, understandably so. It might take years, particularly given other financial pressures a buyer may have.

Another thing to consider is your contingency plan. It's not just the 20 percent down payment you must plan for. Most industry experts recommend also keeping three to six months' worth of mortgage payments in a savings account, just in case something happens. You never know when a job loss, family illness, or unexpected emergency might strap your financial means. Living without a savings account is living on the edge, never knowing if something will happen that might cause you to be late paying your mortgage, which can lead to a financial snowball effect!

Plus, there are closing costs, home insurance, moving costs, and agent fees to consider. Some people don't think of these things and anticipate putting their entire savings into the down payment. Talk about starting off on the wrong foot right from the very beginning!

That said, there may be another disadvantage to waiting until you have saved up enough to make a 20 percent down payment. It might take years to save up that much money, and considering home inflation, the waiting game might not be in your best interest. A smaller down payment could be as little as 5–10 percent, depending on what the lender is prepared to accept based upon your credit score and the type of risk you represent.

So if you are anxious to buy a house without having to wait until the entire 20 percent down payment has been saved, you must weigh the disadvantages accordingly. You will have to pay for private mortgage insurance; your interest rate may be higher; and therefore your monthly mortgage payment will be higher as a result.

DON'T DIG TOO DEEP JUST BECAUSE YOU HAVE A SHOVEL

We've all heard the expression of someone whose "eyes are bigger than their stomach." It refers to someone who fills up a plate of food that is more than they can eat, just because it looks good.

This expression could also apply to the mortgage process. The bank may offer to loan you more than what you are expecting, based upon your financial picture.

Just because the bank is willing to lend you a certain amount— which is disclosed to you during the preapproval process—does not mean that you have to buy a home that costs that much. This is definitely one of the biggest pitfalls to avoid, and I can't stress it enough! If you have a yellow highlighter, dig it out and remember this wisdom. It can be the key difference between enjoyable homeownership versus financial struggles and regret. Happiness is the underlying reason why people want to own their own home, so let's make sure we keep it that way even when it comes to manageability of your finances.

The bank or mortgage professionals are calculating your spending power based on what they see on your credit profile. If you have additional expenditures that are not on your credit report, then chances are the final preapproval amount they give you will be higher than what you can actually afford to spend. For instance, childcare will not show up on your report. If you take care of an elderly family member or if you are paying off a private loan, those things will not be a consideration in reviewing your monthly financial threshold. So you may want to share that information with them up front. Or at the very least, mentally modify the amount to reflect your true financial picture. Let's say you are preapproved for a mortgage that costs $2,800 per month, but you know you have an additional $800 outgoing that has not been accounted for. In this case, you should scale back to a mortgage that will only cost you $2,000 per month.

If a home price seems outside of your means, then go with your instinct. Instead of buying a $300,000 house, for example, perhaps you could find something that still meets your needs in the $200,000 range. It may not have the swimming pool in the backyard, but you can always add enhancements to your property later on when you are financially able. Trust me on this! You'll thank me later.

CHILL PILL #12

Just because the bank thinks you look great on paper does not mean you should borrow all of the funds that they are willing to lend. Why? You're going to have to pay it back with interest! Over-extending yourself is a bad idea. Stick to your original budget.

Let's face it: Most homebuyers finance the majority of their home's purchase price within a mortgage loan. So, consider that whatever amount you put down up front determines the total you must borrow and the subsequent payments each month. Put it all down on paper first, looking at it from a conservative perspective.

As I pointed out earlier in the book, there may be several benefits to purchasing when you have saved enough for a down payment of 20 percent or more. This is just my way of giving you a nudge on the right track to homeownership, but the choice is ultimately yours!

Understandably, the whole process of buying a home comes with many learning experiences. A good real estate broker can walk you through all of the necessary steps, even if it means providing you with a checklist or perhaps discussing these matters prior to searching for the right house. But you may want to start wrapping your mind around some ways you can prepare now to be an attractive homebuyer on paper for the banks. This next chapter should help.

CHAPTER 6

GETTING APPROVED FOR A MORTGAGE:
Which Home Loan is Right for You?

YOU HAVE SAVED AND SAVED YOUR HARD-EARNED dollars and finally have enough for at least a 10 percent or 20 percent down payment. Is it time to start shopping for a home? Well, let's not put the cart before the horse, shall we?

Fear not, you are getting closer to your dream of homeownership. The steps are definitely arduous, but will be well worth it. You will appreciate everything you have gone through once you finally do find the home of your dreams. As the saying goes, *"Anything worth having requires hard work and effort,"* and homeownership is certainly at the top of the list.

FINANCIAL MILESTONES
TO HOMEOWNERSHIP

Let's take a look at the financial milestones you'll need to hit on your road to homeownership:

- **Prequalification.** Getting prequalified is the initial step in the mortgage process, and it's generally fairly simple. You supply a bank or lender with your overall financial picture, including your debt, income, and assets. After evaluating this information, a lender can give you an idea of the mortgage amount for which you qualify. Pre-qualification can be done over the phone or on the internet, and there is usually no cost involved.

- **Preapproval.** Getting preapproved is the next step, and it tends to be much more involved. You'll complete an official mortgage application (and usually pay an application fee), and then supply the lender with the necessary documentation to perform an extensive check on your financial background and current credit rating. (Typically at this stage, you will not have found a house yet, so any reference to "property" on the application will be left blank.) From this, the lender can tell you the specific mortgage amount for which you are preapproved. You'll also have a better idea of the interest rate you will be charged on the loan and, in some cases, you might be able to lock in a specific rate.

With preapproval, you will receive a conditional commitment in writing for an exact loan amount, allowing you to look for a home at or below that price level. Obviously, this puts you at an advantage when dealing with a potential seller, as he or she will know you're one step closer to obtaining an actual mortgage.

CHILL PILL #13

Before you look at any homes, it's best if you go straight to the preapproval process. This way, you won't waste time with guessing or looking at properties that are beyond your means. Getting preapproved also enables you to move quickly when you find the perfect place. In a competitive market, this lets the seller know that your offer is serious—and could prevent you from losing out to another potential buyer who already has financing arranged. If you're going to take time to get pre-qualified, you might as well go a few steps further and go for the preapproval.

• **Mortgage Commitment.** While preapproval is what you obtain *before* you begin searching for a home, the next step—a mortgage commitment—is what you obtain *after* you've found your home and are officially "under contract." A mortgage commitment from a lender means you have submitted a Uniform Residential Loan Application, copy of a photo ID, pay stubs, verification of employment, bank statements, the last two years of your W-2s or 1099 statements, the last two years of your tax returns, and verification of deposits for your down payment. Once the lender's evaluation is completed, they issue a letter verifying your mortgage commitment.

It's important to note that the commitment is based on the income, credit, and other information that was approved. If anything should change, then your commitment can be revoked or amended. This means that you can't stop paying your bills, buy two new cars, or quit your job, and remain approved. No mortgage loan is one hundred percent approved until it is closed.

- **Final Approval.** Once all the property reports are in hand, as well as the additional list of items required for initial underwriting, the file goes *back* to the underwriter for final sign off. (The underwriter is the person/ department at the bank who processes and approves your loan.) At this point, the underwriter could fully sign off on the file as ready to fund, or ask for additional documentation. Remember to keep calm. . . This is normally the step where buyers lose patience. It's fairly common for banks to request further documents or clarification on an item you've already turned in. After they've checked through everything, a final approval letter will specify the amount and type of the loan that's been approved, free of any additional conditions or "subject to's." A final approval, unlike a pre-qualification or preapproval, means your financing has been secured.

EIGHT WAYS TO BE AN
ATTRACTIVE BORROWER ON PAPER

1. **Prove Your Stability.** If you jump around to different jobs faster than the seasons change, then this might alarm the bank. They want to see consistency in your paychecks over a long period of time.

2. **Keep Your Credit Score High.** Be vigilant about not letting your credit score drop. Freecreditreport.com and other sites offer *free* annual credit reports. Generally speaking, it's wise to pull your credit report annually to ensure nothing is reported negatively. Even one small change can alarm the bank. Buyers with credit scores over the 700 mark typically have more leverage in securing the best possible interest rates. You will learn more about credit scores later in this chapter.

3. **Lower Your Debt-to-Credit Ratio.** Even if you have good credit, if you have a lot of credit cards with high maximum limits, this can be a disadvantage for you. Why? Well, when times get tough for people, they often turn to credit cards to get caught up, which can put them further and further behind the eight-ball. Banks would rather see low maximum limits with low balances. I would recommend keeping no more than three or four cards that you use occasionally and then cutting up or paying off the rest.

4. **Save Enough for the Down Payment *and* Closing Costs.** Again, closing costs can equate to approximately 3 to 5 percent of the loan, so saving only enough for the down payment can leave you in a bind, which the bank will view unfavorably.

5. **Pad Your Savings Account, Too!** On paper, this looks great in the eyes of the bank. They will see that you have planned for those "just in case" mishaps that life often brings.

6. **Pay Your Bills on Time.** Do you pay your bills on time or do you accrue late fees even if you have enough money to cover them? Late payments indicate irresponsibility to a mortgage lender. Being busy or forgetful is understandable once in a while, but if payments on your auto, utilities, or credit cards are always late, then banks will consider you at risk for late mortgage payments.

7. **Have Your Paperwork Ready.** Being organized and having proof of your job stability, income, and credit history ready in advance shows the bank that you are a serious homebuyer who is also prepared to take homeownership seriously.

8. **Be Accurate.** Make sure none of your paperwork has been falsified or is outdated. Banks want the most recent and up-to-date information about you to make their decision.

WHAT IS A CREDIT SCORE, AND WHY IS IT IMPORTANT?

A credit score is a number from 0 to 850, used by lenders to determine whether you are a risky or a great candidate for them to extend a loan. People who have financial problems often have lower scores because they are unable to keep up with their bills. They fall behind on payments, make late payments, or sometimes ditch their financial obligations altogether since they are unable to pay them back.

The FICO credit score is the one most creditors use. It includes three organizations that offer a combined number to tally your score. They are Equifax, TransUnion, and Experian. Everyone is entitled to a free credit score once each year. Additionally, you can often get one through your bank for free.

TEN WAYS TO IMPROVE YOUR CREDIT AND SCORE YOURSELF THE BEST MORTGAGE

One of the major factors in buying a new house is your credit score. Even if everything seems okay, it's best to check beforehand and gear up for this financial transition. Here are ten ways to keep your credit score high:

1. **Pay on Time.** Paying bills on time accounts for a major amount of your score, which is determined by the Fair Isaac Corporation. It is a system and not a person, and therefore doesn't take into account that you had a bump in the road that caused the late payment.

2. **Keep Your Debt-to-Credit Ratio at 30 percent.** What does this mean? If you have a credit card with a limit of $2,000, make sure you do not carry a balance over $600.

3. **Pay Things Off.** If you want to increase your score and are able to pay something off—even something small—do so. This brings your credit score *up*! So take a look at that car loan. If you only have a couple of grand left to pay it off, why not use your tax refund to improve your credit and feel great about having one less payment every month?

4. **Dispute Wrongdoings.** Credit card companies are notorious for errors, so if you spot something on your credit report that is not true, you can absolutely contest it. Many people do not take the time to look or to dispute things even when they feel as though they have been wronged. It helps if you keep documentation, but generally you are allowed to have at least one faulty transaction taken off your record each year.

5. **Tackle Credit Card Debt.** It can be good to have a few credit cards that you pay responsibly, but if you open up your wallet and twenty cards fall out, it might be time to

whittle down that debt. Make a list of what you owe on each card and start paying them down. Tackle the smaller and more recent cards first, and then close those accounts after they are paid. Keep the long-standing cards, but get them down to that 30 percent ratio I mentioned in Tip #2.

6. **Show Variety.** Just when I tell you to get rid of some of those cards, now I'm telling you to mix it up. Hear me out . . . If you have only one bill for $5,000 and another person has three bills equaling the same amount and you are both paying on time, the second person is more likely to have a higher score. So spread your credit card use around.

7. **Clear Up Past Bank Problems.** If you have ever stiffed a bank that charged you a lot of fees for one bounced check that spiraled out of control, rather than letting the account drop and never going back to the bank, you must make amends. The money you owe will affect your ability to open any future accounts with other banks because the default shows on the system (seemingly forever).

8. **Stay Put.** Stability is a good way to show that you are fiscally responsible, so if you move around a lot, it actually harms your credit. Of course, this isn't necessarily your fault. You may find a job that requires you to move. Life situations arise (which they do!), but this is one more tip you can store in your memory bank.

9. Avoid Credit Card Offers. It's tempting when you receive "No Interest" offers to transfer balances to another card, but read the fine print before you do. Jumping from one credit card company to another can actually harm your credit.

10. Say "No" to Incentive Sign-Ups. When you go to department stores, the sales clerk will frequently ask you to save 10 percent or more on your purchase by signing up for a store card. Not only does this hurt your credit with extra inquiries, but having more cards will have a negative impact on your score.

CHILL PILL #14

Disputing things on your credit report places the burden of proof on the creditor, so if you feel that you have been wronged, you should absolutely try to get it amended! It also doesn't hurt to put a fraud protection alert on your credit report. This makes it so that no one can open accounts in your name without a security code. It's a great protection from fraud!

HOW TO AVOID DAMAGING
YOUR CREDIT SCORE

Before you try to improve your credit score, you must find out exactly what the score is. Sometimes people ruin their scores without meaning to, often thinking they are improving it by certain actions. For example, canceling a credit card can actually damage your score if the card has a high limit and low balance. Sounds a bit ridiculous, but credit bureaus use a calculation of your available credit versus how much you owe to help determine the score, which means that canceling that card can then increase your debt-to-credit ratio.

Another surprising way your credit score can be harmed is by forgetting to take a book back to the library. A simple, yet seemingly harmless $15 book can lower your score by as much as a hundred points! That is only if the library reports the book to a collection agency, which in some cities they do.

Many people find past medical bills coming back to haunt them. That trip you took to the emergency room a few years ago and forgot to pay can cost you a lot of points. Hospitals and medical facilities almost always report past-due balances. It's better to work out a payment arrangement if you cannot pay for the services at the time it happened. I know a person whose $1,400 medical bill from years before caused him to get rejected for a traditional loan, and therefore he had to pay a much higher interest rate. You can see now how some of these minor delinquencies can be detrimental, especially when you are talking about the difference between paying a 3.5 percent interest rate versus a 6 percent interest rate on a mortgage. In the long run, it will equal thousands of dollars more than it would have cost you to simply work out a payment arrangement with the hospital.

But the worst factor that will cost you major points is paying bills late. According to the way scores are calculated, you're sending a message that collecting payments will be problematic for them.

How can you avoid these seemingly innocent catastrophes? Call the company you owe and work out a payment arrangement. That way you cannot be penalized for being a few days late and you will still continue making a concerted effort to keep your credit score as high as possible.

CHILL PILL #15

If you think that paying back past credit card debt from a few years ago will help you, think again! Once your debt has been charged-off (written off as a lost cause) by a credit card company, any recent activity, like paying the debt down, will make your debts appear recent, too. The scoring system will then penalize you. Not fair, but true! It takes seven years to wipe a negative mark off your credit report, so ride it out if it has been close to that long. However, if you have any charge-offs that are more recent (say, within the past year or so), then try to work out an arrangement.

EENIE-MEENIE-MINEY MORTGAGE: WHICH HOME LOAN IS RIGHT FOR YOU?

Let's say you have already gone through the preapproval process. You're excited because the bank told you that you have "buying power" of up to $300,000. Whoopee! You start looking at homes in the $300k price range. *Wait a minute,* the voice of reason whispers in your ear. *Isn't there more to this?* Then it starts tapping you on the shoulder, and finally it tries to get your attention in other ways.

Before you start bidding on your dream home, a bit more busywork is in order. You already know to factor in the taxes, insurance, and closing costs. But what's the bottom line going to be each month? It all depends on your mortgage.

Determining which mortgage is best for your circumstances is probably one of the most common questions asked by those who are in the market to purchase a home. There are conventional, variable rates, ARM loans, and FHA or VA loans to choose from. Eenie, Meenie, Miney, Mortgage! So how do you determine which is right for you?

Basically, it comes down to just a few things. Do you prefer a mortage whose rate is higher but will stay the same, or is lower to start with but may vary over time? Do you want a conventional or government-backed loan?

Just a few years ago, during the housing boom, there were enough mortgage options to make your head spin. During that period, lenders were essentially tailoring their mortgage products to suit the borrower, whether they were qualified or not. Those were the days of money-back loans and zero due at closing. The subprime lending disaster ultimately led to the housing crash and foreclosure crisis.

These days, however, the government has placed more stringent restrictions on the lending world. Those riskier mortgages are no longer an option and most lenders primarily require a 10 to 20 percent down payment. Although they're now tougher to get than they used to be, people have become wiser about them through making sound financial decisions and by knowing their options.

So, what are some of the different types of mortgages? The three most common mortgages are FHA loans, VA loans, and conventional loans:

- **FHA Loans:** An FHA loan is a government-insured loan offered to first-time homebuyers. Federal Housing Administration–approved lenders provide loans aimed at first-time buyers' special needs. These loans offer higher loan-to-value rates, fixed or adjustable interest rates, and less-demanding requirements for income and down payments than conventional loans. For instance, the FHA permits first-time buyers to borrow up to 97 percent of the value of the property. When people talk about 3 to 3.5 percent down options, they are referring to an FHA loan.

- **VA Loans**: A VA loan is also a government-backed loan, but this particular loan is overseen by the Department of

Veterans Affairs. It was designed solely for American veterans and their spouses. It allows US veterans to purchase a home with no down payment and 103.3 percent financing without private mortgage insurance. The additional 3.3 percent is to cover closing costs.

- **Conventional Loans**: A conventional loan is neither made by a government entity, nor insured by a government entity. It's what we refer to as a non-GSE (non-government sponsored entity) loan. A conventional, or conforming, mortgage can be backed by a bank, credit union, or savings and loan association and adheres to the guidelines set by Fannie Mae and Freddie Mac, that is, the Federal National Mortgage Association and Federal Home Loan Mortgage Corporation. A conventional mortgage may have either a fixed or adjustable rate.

WHAT ARE THE DIFFERENCES BETWEEN FHA, VA, AND CONVENTIONAL LOANS?

The main difference between these loans is who can qualify for them, as defined above. Down payment requirements are different as well. The minimum down payment for an FHA loan is 3.5 percent. For a VA loan, the minimum down payment is zero. For a conventional loan you can expect anywhere from 5 percent down to 20 percent down. However, with conventional loans, if you put less than 20 percent down on your mortgage, you'll get hit with something called PMI, or private mortgage insurance, which was mentioned in Chapter 5. It can add thousands of dollars on top of your annual mortgage expense. If you put down less than 20 percent on your conventional loan, you will have to pay monthly PMI until you have built up enough equity in your home that the lender no longer considers you a risk. With PMI, the higher your loan, the more you pay.

Within the conventional loan perameters, you will have the option of a fixed-rate or an adjustable rate:

- **Fixed-Rate Mortgage:** Fixed-rate mortgages are also referred to as "conventional loans." With the fixed-rate option, you'll have the same interest rate for the entire life of the loan. This is true whether you keep the loan for fifteen or thirty years. Keep in mind that your mortgage payment can still change even with a fixed-rate. This is normally caused by an increase or decrease in taxes, insurance, or escrow. However, the guaranteed fixed interest rate will always remain the same for the life of the loan.

- **Adjustable-Rate Mortgage:** An adjustable-rate mortgage, commonly known as an ARM mortgage, is the direct opposite of the fixed-rate loan. The interest rate fluctuates over the life of the loan, depending on market conditions. It can go up or down, but I have very rarely seen it go down, except after the housing bust, when mortgage rates hit record lows. It's the exception, not the rule. To sum it up, an ARM mortgage means that your overall mortgage payment is guaranteed to change in some capacity over the life of the loan.

- **Mixed-Rate Mortgage:** Some people also call these "combo" loans or hybrids. You may see lenders offer 5/1 ARM, 7/1 ARM, or 10/1 ARM mortgages. The idea is that the bank mirrors the fixed-rate conventional loan for a set period of time (the first number in the term), and begins to adjust after that time expires. Personally speaking, I once had a 7/1 ARM mortgage at 5.75 percent. The interest rate remained the same for the first seven years of the loan, and then began adjusting every year after the seventh year. Eventually, my mortgage rate would have been over 8 percent, had I not been ready to sell and move into another home.

You may be wondering why anyone would choose an ARM or mixed loan versus a guaranteed fixed-rate. The simple answer is that combo mortgages generally offer a lower interest rate than a fixed-rate loan, at least in the beginning. Some homebuyers prefer a lower monthly payment during the first few years of homeownership, so they opt for the ARM. Also, if you don't plan on staying in the home for a long period of time, it may make sense to choose an ARM mortgage. If you know that you plan to move in eight years or that your home purchase is not your permanent residence, then a 10/1 ARM mortgage makes perfect sense because you will be able to get out of the home and move into the next one before the rate adjusts.

These days, I tend to prefer fixed-rate mortgages. After all, nobody likes unpleasant surprises when it comes to interest rates. Seven years can seem like a long ways away, but it goes by fast! You may appreciate the security of a guaranteed fixed interest rate loan. While it's true that you will pay a higher rate than the initial rate on an ARM loan, at least you won't have to guess. That's like trying to guess which horse will win a race for you next year. What if the horse gets injured? It's better to put your money on a sure bet than to gamble with fluctuating terms.

At the time of this book's publication, interest rates are still at all-time lows, so it makes perfect sense to lock into a low, fixed-rate. Ultimately, you will have to decide which mortgage product suits your needs and lifestyle.

Now, let's go back to talk more about FHA loans. If you're a first-time homebuyer, this may be just the ticket for you. In fact, the rules for who is a first-time buyer may be less strict than you think:

- According to the Internal Revenue Service, you can be considered a "first-time" homebuyer if it has been three or more years since you owned a home. This rule only applies if the property will be your place of residency. It does *not* apply to investment properties.

- If you are separated or divorced from your spouse, you can also qualify as a first-time homebuyer, according to the Federal Housing Administration. One of the qualifiers is whether you have ever owned a home with your spouse (the spouse has to be on the deed, as well). You must also be a single parent or a displaced homemaker.

- If you have only owned a primary residence that wasn't permanently connected to land, such as a mobile home, you would be considered a first-time homebuyer, according to the FHA.

- You would also be considered a first-time homebuyer if you've owned property that wasn't up to code and would cost more to repair than to rebuild. Just as with the mobile home, it must be the only property you've owned.

- According to the IRS, minors are generally not considered purchasers of a home and therefore don't qualify as first-time homebuyers. The one exception is when the minor is married. Even then, the minor's spouse must be over eighteen to meet the criteria.

WHAT IS A GRADUATED PAYMENT LOAN?

FHA and VA loans aren't the only options for a low-interest-rate loan. Another option for low income buyers is the graduated payment loan.

Graduated payment mortgages are an alternative to conventional loans for low-income buyers who expect their income to grow in the next five to ten years. Payments start so low they don't even cover the interest on the loan, but they increase each year. This program allows individuals to apply for a mortgage much sooner than they would be able to through a conventional mortgage.

WHAT IS A HOME EQUITY LOAN?

In essence, home equity loans are second mortgages. Once you actually own a home, a loan can be taken out against the value of your property in addition to your primary mortgage. These loans can offer great benefits, but they certainly come attached with some large risks, as well.

Home equity loans or home equity lines of credit are based on the amount of equity you have built up in your home. For instance, if your mortgage balance is $150,000 but your home's value is $225,000, then you have $75,000 worth of equity in the home and would more than likely be eligible for a home equity loan.

The advantages of these types of loans are that they allow homeowners to borrow a large sum of cash against the value of their home, with the flexibility to use it for any purpose. Many people use second home loans for things like debt consolidation, home improvement, avoiding private mortgage insurance (PMI), paying for college tuition, and investing in other properties. Other loans just aren't big enough to cover these types of expenses.

Another advantage of home equity loans is that they are considered safer by lenders than other types. Why? Because they are secured by the house. In other words, banks will actually get something back if you default on the loan. On the bright side, borrowers can usually land much lower interest rates on second mortgages than on unsecured loans or credit cards.

Oh, and there are tax benefits in choosing second mortgages, as compared with other loans. The interest for a second mortgage is tax deductible, unlike the interest from a credit card balance, for instance.

DISADVANTAGES OF SECOND MORTGAGES

You knew it was coming, didn't you? Even though banks consider second mortgages "safer" than traditional mortgages, there are still some major drawbacks involved with borrowing additional money against your house. Most significantly, second loans are risky because if the homeowner is unable to repay the loan for whatever reason (like getting in over his head), he risks losing the house to foreclosure and in turn, ruining his credit. The risk of foreclosure does not exist with other unsecured loans. The hazards of a second loan should make borrowers seriously consider whether they really need the large loan.

Also important to note: Second loans require fees and closing costs, just like first mortgages. You may also be required to pay points (one point is equal to one percent of the loan value), which could make the loan less attractive. And while second mortgage rates are certainly better than credit card rates, they are still higher than first mortgage loans. This is because the first mortgage takes precedence over the second in terms of repayment, in the case of default.

Second mortgages can be a great way to access lower-cost funding for certain major financial ventures, as long as borrowers do not overreach by taking out more money than they can comfortably afford to repay.

Whether we're talking about first or second mortgages, be sure to shop for low-cost loans among mortgage lenders. Banks want your business, but they are not so eager to part with the money for the loan. They want to make sure they recover their money and that you will be dependable in repaying it. They know that you want to buy a home and live in it, and that having a home is the most important bill you will pay each month. Somehow, the process is often complicated—no matter how great you look on paper.

CHILL PILL #16

Don't forget to consider the taxes and insurance on your mortgage expense to avoid getting stuck with untimely bills. The mortgage company will typically include this within your monthly payments so that you pay throughout the year.

CHAPTER 7

THE THRILL OF MAKING AN OFFER:
How to Seal the Deal

LET ME TELL YOU A LITTLE SECRET. COME A LITTLE
closer. When I visit houses with a client, I can tell very
quickly whether or not the home is a good fit. They'll say
things like:

> *"Oh, honey . . . look at that tree in the backyard! It will be
> fun for you to install a swing or build a treehouse for the
> kids there."*

> *"Our king-size mahogany bed will look so amazing in this
> master bedroom!"*

"Let's paint this room blue. My Navajo rug will look great in the middle of the room."

You see, when people truly love a house, they start to picture themselves living in it. They picture their own belongings in the rooms, or they envision their family participating in activities on the grounds. They can imagine where things go or how they'll decorate to make it tailored to their own preferences and styles. That is how I can tell when we have picked out a winner . . . a *gem property*! And when that gem property comes at a price that is exactly within their budget or lower, even better!

When that silent, internal nudge to make an offer kicks in . . . act quickly! This is the point at which your real estate agent should try not to dissuade you, but rather guide you through the next phase of the home-buying process and help boost your confidence as you take this next big step toward homeownership. It's time to make an offer.

Once you have made the decision to make an offer, the next move is for your real estate agent to call the listing agent who represents the home you're interested in. Their role at this juncture is to ask the right questions to gauge the situation. How motivated is the seller? Have there been any other offers on the table? Based upon the feedback you receive via your buyer's agent, you'll be better armed with facts necessary to create an offer strategy that will ultimately put you in the most desirable position as a buyer for that particular home.

At this point, your bidding strategy options are two-fold:

• Proceed to make a lower offer with the hopes that the seller will accept your bid or at the very least counter you with a number that is not too far off from your initial offer.

- Cut to the chase and offer the seller a price close to the asking price, if not at the full price.

Bear in mind that the deciding factor on which option you choose largely depends on the level of supply versus the demand for that particular style of home in that condition in a given area during the same time period. And of course the game changes if other offers have also been made.

Now you may gasp when reading this. You may be wondering, why in the world would Egypt suggest I even consider paying full asking price for a home? Well, if you've watched me go through the home-buying process on my show, *Property Virgins*, then you're no stranger to the many "bidding wars" I've had to wage on behalf of my clients. I'm proud to say I've won most of the bidding wars I've participated in. However, there have been those instances when certain clients felt they knew more than I do (despite my being the real estate expert), and they opted to "play hardball" by assuming they were the only buyers in the market.

Eventually, their dreams were shattered when they were outbid by another buyer who recognized a good house when they saw it and acted accordingly.

HOW TO WIN THE
BATTLE IN A BIDDING WAR:
FIVE TIPS TO HELP YOU SUCCEED

Even if another buyer has made an offer on the house you want, keep calm. This does not mean that you are out of the running. While a multiple-offer situation may put the seller in a more powerful position than the potential buyers, it doesn't mean you need to panic. What it does mean is that there's a possibility you may have to pay more for that particular home than you anticipated. You will also have to be more flexible than some of the other buyers to put yourself in the most favorable position with the seller.

If this is the house of your dreams, aren't you willing to fight for it? Don't dwell on the fact that you could have made an offer sooner. Let the bidding war begin, my friends! Your sword is your trusty pen!

While offering the most money might seem like the best way to win a bidding war, sellers don't always choose the highest offer. Instead, sellers often prefer offers that are most likely to go through and that meet their conditions. For instance, if your lease is expiring in the next sixty days and you're in a rush to get to the closing table, but the seller wants ninety days to move because they haven't yet found the new home they plan to purchase and move into, the seller may be inclined to take a slightly lower offer from a more flexible buyer rather than the higher bid you put in.

Keep your eyes on the prize. Stay focused, and don't give up the fight. To help arm you with the leverage you need to be victorious in this battle, I'm going to give you five ways to succeed at a bidding war to buy the house you truly want.

1. **Have all your paperwork in order.** Sellers want to know where your money is coming from. When submitting your offer, be prepared to show your preapproval mortgage eligibility letter showing the amount you are approved for. It must be at least as much as you are offering to pay for the house. If you intend to pay cash for the house, you will need a POF (proof of funds) certified letter or bank statement verifying that you have enough liquid funds available to purchase the home. This shows the seller that you're serious and have all your ducks in a row.

2. **Forget lowball offers–make your best offer now!** In today's climate where housing inventory shortages seem prevalent all across the country, by the time you get in to view a home, there may often be one or more offers on the table. You may only have one shot to get this right, so don't be coy. Make your best offer now! Have your buyer's agent do the research on recent sale prices of comparable properties in the neighborhood, and go for it!

3. **The personal touch goes a long way.** Try to separate yourself from all the other paper offers by personalizing it. Write a letter to the homeowner telling them why you love the house so much. Give them some background information about yourself. Even adding a family photo to the

top of the offer has worked for a few of my buyers over the years. It's often more difficult to say no to someone you feel you know versus a complete stranger.

4. **Eliminate or reduce contingencies.** One of the best ways to make your offer stronger is to eliminate contingencies. If you're a first-time homebuyer, you may not be in a position to waive a mortgage contingency like a more seasoned buyer. However, if you are a veteran buyer who is re-entering the marketplace for a second, third, or maybe even a fourth time, you may have large cash reserves on hand that show that you could in fact purchase a house outright in lieu of getting a mortgage. This could make you more attractive to a seller tasked with making the tough decision of which offer to take.

Now of course, I am not encouraging you to run out and put up your savings or 401K retirement accounts as collateral to purchase a home you really should be getting a mortgage on. What I am saying is this: If you know beyond a shadow of a doubt that your credit profile is up to par, your bank statements are in order, your income-to-debt ratio is not out of whack, and you can show proof of sufficient employment (all of which would make you mortage-worthy), you could consider leveraging your cash status to your benefit to come out on top in a bidding war.

5. **Be very flexible!** Being flexible on the terms of the agreement can give you a leg up. Something as simple as allowing the seller to determine the closing date is a small courtesy

that could make a big difference when trying win over an uncertain seller.

By the way, bidding wars can get emotional quickly, especially if you've fallen in love with a home. It's important to remain mindful of your financial limitations. Devise a "walkaway number" upfront. That dollar amount represents the highest price you'd be willing to pay for that home. Always have the number in the back of your mind so that you know when it's time to move on.

ADD THIS MEMBER TO YOUR REAL ESTATE DREAM TEAM: LAWYER UP!

I get the question in almost every real estate transaction I am involved in: "Egypt, do I really need to hire an attorney?" The answer is both simple and complex. Every state has different requirements. Some states leave it as an option to the buyer and seller, while others mandate it as a necessity.

Your local real estate agent should be able to advise you on the protocol in the area in which you are buying. That's the simple answer. The complex answer has to do with your particular situation. For most people, their home is the biggest purchase they'll ever make. They sign mountains of paperwork for both the loan and the property itself. In a good number of cases, they don't have their own attorney and everything goes smoothly. Other times, an attorney's fee more than pays for itself.

If legal issues arise that your real estate agent can't answer, you'll need an attorney's help. Although good agents know a lot about the negotiating and contracting part of the process, they can't make judgments on legal questions.

For example, what if your prospective new home has an in-law unit with an existing tenant whom you want to evict in order to rent the place to a friend? Only a lawyer can tell you with any certainty whether your plans are feasible. Or, if you're drafting any unusual language for the purchase contract, or are concerned about some language in your mortgage, you may want to have an attorney look the documents over.

A good real estate attorney can also relieve you from some of the frustrations of the buying process. You can dish some of the duties off to your attorney. "Call my lawyer," you can tell the bank representative if there's a question you don't have the answer to. Isn't it nice to have someone on your professional team who is looking out for you?

Your real estate agent has your back, but when they don't have the answers to your legal questions, you can call your real estate attorney to get the answers you need.

HERE ARE SOME OTHER CONSIDERATIONS FOR HIRING A REAL ESTATE ATTORNEY:

Buyers

• Are you an out-of-town buyer?

- Are you buying a property that is a short sale or bank-owned?

- Are you buying a property that is part of an estate sale?

- Are you buying a commercial property?

- Are you buying a property that could potentially have structural issues?

- Are you buying a property in a problematic area such as a flood zone or areas with adverse conditions (tornado prone, or with high radon or toxicity levels)?

Sellers

- Are you selling a property that is in some state of distress?

- Are you the heir or executor of a property whose owner is now deceased?

- Are you selling a house with a non-cooperative partner?

- Do you have that gut feeling that something could possibly go wrong based on your knowledge of the property?

- Do you have judgments or liens in your background?

If you answered yes to any of the above questions, then hiring an attorney to guide you through the process would definitely be beneficial. If none of those apply to you and you have discussed your situation with your realtor, then it's probably fine to use your realtor's knowledge and expertise to take you through to closing. Rest assured, as part of a realtor's licensing education, we are taught about and tested on the real estate contracts used within the state that holds our license.

Another question I am often asked is, "My best friend's cousin is an attorney and would do it for me either free or at low cost. Can I use him? He's not a real estate attorney, but an attorney is an attorney, right?" *wrong*!

You wouldn't go to a gynecologist for a heart valve replacement, would you? Of course not! Nor would you go to a neurosurgeon to have a root canal. Even though they are all doctors who have taken the Hippocratic Oath, they don't specialize in the same type of medical care. Selecting a real estate attorney is no different.

The agreement of sale in a real estate transaction is possibly the single most important piece of the entire deal. It is the legally binding document that pulls together all components, obligations, and covenants associated with a real estate deal. *Do not* hire any old attorney who has a general title. Find a legitimate and experienced real estate attorney who specializes in real estate law, and who performs real estate transactions day in and day out. Even if you have a family lawyer who handles most of your personal and individual matters, this person or firm may not be the best person to hire for your real estate transaction unless, of course, they handle real estate law.

I have seen scenarios where "Uncle Gus," a general attorney, makes changes to the contract in an effort to protect the buyer that are not reasonable. This inflames the seller and the whole transaction blows up. By using a non-real estate specific attorney, you put yourself at great risk of potential financial loss and even possible litigation.

From the latter part of 2010 until the present day, many regulations have been put in place to protect homeowners and banks alike. When contracts come into play, it's important to go with a pro and more importantly, a specialist. Purchasing a home is the type of business transaction that requires an advanced understanding of the real estate laws, rules, and procedures by someone who stays up-to-date on the many changes within the industry.

In some states, a real estate attorney takes over *after* the selling price and terms have been established by the realtors in the contract and all parties have signed. He will review the contract itself, negotiate repairs based on the home inspection report, and collaborate with the title company. He will also be with you at settlement along with your realtor and possibly your lending agent. All of these people are working for you to make sure you are protected.

HOW MUCH DOES A
REAL ESTATE ATTORNEY COST?

Depending on where you live, hiring a real estate attorney typically costs from $800 to $1,500. Compare the costs in your specific area by calling around for estimates. For die-hard bargain shoppers who are always trying to disprove the adage *"you get what you pay for,"* I wish you good luck with Uncle Gus. If it were me, this is one area I wouldn't want to take my chances.

HOW DO I HIRE A GOOD ATTORNEY?

Hiring a real estate lawyer might sound like an easy thing to do. It's as simple as going on your computer and typing "real estate attorney" in your web browser, along with your zip code, right? *Wrong*!

Hiring a solid real estate lawyer is not the same as buying a new bedroom set on Overstock.com. The seemingly endless choices might appear similar in comparison, but making a good choice requires more thought than whether or not to go with a king or queen, or pink versus tan and periwinkle blue. Instead of searching for a deal on a prospective lawyer, you should hire the best real estate attorney for the job, making sure they are one that you can afford.

Referrals and recommendations may be your best source for finding a person in your local area. Your real estate agent is probably knowledgeable and has worked with many different lawyers over the years. They often know who is best and whose face they see most often at the closing table. If your agent doesn't have anyone in mind, then consider recommendations from colleagues at work, family members, friends, or neighbors who have recently purchased or sold homes. Ask if they were happy with the way the real estate attorney handled their transaction, and inquire whether they would recommend this person without reservation.

Once you have narrowed it down to two or three options, take advantage of the free consultation many lawyers offer. Find out their prices, what is included in their services, what to expect in terms of their involvement, and how they will serve you!

I've pretty much summed up the offer-making process, and what role certain players on your home-buying team play. Next, you'll meet another person who should absolutely be on your dream team personnel list! This person is so important that I've decided to devote a whole chapter to what they do . . . so read on!

CHAPTER 8

GET OUT YOUR MAGNIFYING GLASS:

Why You Should Never Overlook the Inspection

THERE IS ONE MORE "VIP" WHO WILL BECOME AN integral part of your professional guidance team. Who is it? Would you care for some clues?

Think of Sherlock Holmes with his magnifying glass. Or the beloved 1980s cartoon character, Inspector Gadget, with all of his long limbs and useful tools. Still stumped?

It's your home inspector! Hiring a home inspector will be one of the smartest things you've ever done in your life. They have a knack for "getting to the bottom of things" by discovering problems that others may have overlooked.

I love a bargain as much as the next person, but I learned more than a decade ago when I purchased my first investment property that getting a home inspection is one thing you *must not* cut corners on. Even if it seems like yet another $400 to $800 tacked on to your already mounting tally of closing expenses, this is a relatively modest amount of money to spend in comparison to the headaches and financial beatings you may face if the house ends up being a "lemon." Have you ever seen the comedy with Tom Hanks, *The Money Pit*? Unfortunately, this scenario happens all over the United States every day, and the people who were once happy new homeowners are certainly not laughing.

Let me give you an example of why I am so adamant about the home inspection. I once had a cash buyer whom I will call *Mr. Know-It-All*. Maybe you know the type: the guy with deep pockets and an expert at every profession under the sun, from carpentry, waterproofing, electrical work, and plumbing to roofing and landscaping. You name it, and he proclaimed to be an "expert" at it.

For more than a year and a half, I worked to find a transitional home for this bachelor who was moving out of a condo and into the residential lifestyle. He wanted a place with lots of personality in a "hip" neighborhood, but at the same time he wanted it to be a good investment property to put his money into for the long run. Without exaggeration, I believe I showed him close to fifty properties! I worked hard for him in every way imaginable, and found one great deal after the next. However, nothing was good enough for him. Just as we were both ready to throw in the towel on finding him the perfect house to buy, *Eureka . . . we struck gold!*

Indeed, I found him a nearly 3,000-square-foot, four-bedroom, two-and-a-half-bath single-family home located on a quiet cul-de-sac in an up-and-coming neighborhood. The home was within walking distance to a top-rated elementary school, so I knew immediately that this house was a real gem and offered incredible resale potential. Ultimately, that was what he wanted: a home he could live in and then flip for a sizable profit in a few years.

Even though he liked it instantly, the work was not over. After showing it to him on six different occasions (yes, you saw that right—six!), my client finally got to the stage in which he was willing to write an offer on the property. Hallelujah. Can anyone say, "Happy Hour?!"

That Saturday, my client came to my real estate office, and as we sat and talked over a cup of coffee, we reviewed all of the legal paperwork that is required to present an offer to purchase. I had prepared a custom Comparative Market Analysis (CMA) for us to review and discuss.

CHILL PILL #18

Ask your real estate agent to give you a comparative market analysis (CMA) prior to submitting an offer on any property. A CMA averages out the selling price of recently sold homes in the area that are similar to yours. This is a valuable negotiating tool.

Why, you may ask? A thoroughly researched CMA gives buyers and their real estate agents an accurate perspective on what the most recent sales have been in the area. It looks at prices for similar homes within certain neighborhoods or within a half mile radius of the perspective home. Armed with a CMA, the buyer will be far less apt to overpay for a property. This way, instead of "Mr. Know-It-All" using his all-knowing gut feelings and spidey senses to come up with a good offer, we actually used real-time factual sales data to back up our hunches.

Keep in mind that the list price of the particular house that he had looked at half a dozen times was impacted by the low supply and high demand trends that were prevalent at that time. By the time he finally got around to making an offer, there were four other prospective buyers who put forth proposals to purchase the very same home.

Wouldn't you know it, after intense negotiations between my client, me, the seller, and the seller's agent, Mr. Know-It-All's bid was the one they accepted! My client was relieved and eager to get to the closing table so that he could vacate his rented condo and occupy his new home.

At that point, I was just as excited for him to move into the home as he was. However, just as I do with all of my clients, I urged him to get a home inspection performed by a professionally licensed and certified inspector. In his offer, we did not waive his right to an inspection, so he was well within his right to do so. But Mr. Know-It-All was rather annoyed that he had wound up in a bidding war to buy the property. Annoyance turned into impatience, and he dismissed the notion of needing to get a home inspection. In his eyes, it was an unnecessary expense that would prolong his month-to-month condo lease and further delay his impending move. No matter how much I begged and pleaded with him throughout the course of ten days, he refused to budge.

"I appreciate your guidance as my agent," he insisted, "but I know everything there is to know about the makeup of a house , and this one needs nothing more than some basic cosmetic work."

"Okay, okay . . ." I replied. And what more could I do? According to the contract, we had only four days left to complete the home inspection, or Mr. Know-It-All would then forfeit his right to have one conducted prior to closing. As a last-ditch effort, I had one of the top home inspectors in the real estate business give my client a call to give him a candid outlook on the possible pitfalls of skipping an inspection. This, too, went in one ear and out the other. My buyer refused yet again.

Eventually, I came to the conclusion that I couldn't change his mind, and conceded to his decision. Then the real drama began.

After a quick closing on the house, my client officially became the new owner of an amazing home. *Screeeee-e-e-ech! Not so fast.*

At first, everything went swimmingly. I called my client a couple of times during the week after closing to make sure he was still enjoying his new digs and asked if there was anything of concern or items that he needed help with in the home.

All was fine and dandy until he got to week number five. I remember it like it was yesterday. At approximately 8:15 a.m. on a rainy Sunday morning, I was startled out of my peaceful slumber by my cell phone ringing nonstop. I hit "ignore" and put the phone on vibrate, but the caller was persistent. Finally, I picked up.

"Hello?" I said, perturbed.

Wouldn't you know it? Mr. Know-It-All was calling, and he was heated! I could almost see the fire breathing through the receiver as he yelled.

Apparently he was in Asia on a business trip, and while his housekeeper was at his house to do her bi-weekly cleaning, she discovered nearly two feet of water rising in his basement. The sump pump that was supposed to turn on automatically to suction water off the floor, never turned itself on. A torrential storm had caused a power outage on the entire block. Although the outage was temporary for most of the neighborhood, at my client's house the electricity never came back on. And without him being there, he was unaware of the problem.

Once he hastily returned home from his business trip, Mr. Know-It-All discovered an electrical problem with the circuit breaker panel that had been installed by the previous owner of the house. When the storm tripped the electrical box, the power never kicked back on, while the other homes nearby got their power back right away. From that instant, there was a domino effect of one problem after the next.

With no power on in the house, all of the food in his refrigerator had defrosted and gone bad. Then the water from the frozen items that dethawed leaked out of the freezer onto the hardwood floors in his kitchen and ruined them.

I never like to be the one to say, "I told you so," but in the back of my mind, I remembered begging and pleading with this guy many times to get a home inspection. Although the homeowners insurance covered most of the damage, he now had a $20,000 repair tab and had to take off a week from his job to oversee the work being done. This catastrophe could have easily been avoided if he just listened in the first place and gotten a home inspection.

The moral of the story is this: I always tell my Property Virgins to *never* skip the home inspection! It is a crucial part of purchasing your home. Home inspections are designed to protect you from unexpected repairs and costs after move-in. If any problems are found during a pre-sale inspection, the buyer can then negotiate with the seller to have the issues resolved before closing, or to incorporate the cost of repairs into the offer.

CHILL PILL #19

The $300–400 you pay for a home inspection up front can save you loads of time, money, and heartache on the back end. Charge it off as one of the necessary costs associated with purchasing a home. As Nike says, *just do it*!

YOUR SECRET NEGOTIATING WEAPON

Many buyers get caught up in the emotional aspects of a home and overlook common flaws or imperfections as they see only the best features. This makes it nearly impossible for them to anticipate any problems with the house prior to making an offer, and sometimes the buyers waive the right to an inspection altogether. While a home inspection is not a foolproof method of avoiding problems, it does become a great tool for negotiation.

Just for that fact alone, hiring a home inspector is worth it. A licensed professional inspector can pinpoint things that need replacing, servicing, repairing, or redoing altogether. The few hundred dollars it will cost for the services will arm you with a powerful tool to bring to the closing table.

A home inspection is an evaluation that occurs when the prospective buyer hires a licensed individual to go to the property for a thorough walk-through to determine the physical, mechanical, structural, and cosmetic condition of the house. The inspector's role is to be unbiased and offer an impartial perspective, often pointing out things that you should be aware of in advance so that you're not caught off guard down the road. Such items might set you back financially or even pose potential hazards. Getting them taken care of before closing is in your best interest. After the deed is in your name, it's too late!

I should make it clear that your inspector should *not* be anyone close to you, such as a friend, relative, or family acquaintance, unless they are certified and bonafide. Even if your friend happens to be a builder or a contractor by trade, this doesn't save you money in the long run. Building contractors are different than licensed home inspectors. So although they may be qualified to notice a few things, there are many unique points that a professional licensed inspector will cover with meticulous observation.

The home inspector's purpose is to explain to their client what the condition of the house is in its current state—both interior and exterior qualities—as well as the good and bad that he finds. By knowing about these qualities ahead of time, you can request that some of the repairs be done prior to purchasing the house. I should also make it clear that the inspector's job is not to give you advice as to whether or not you should buy the property; he or she merely remarks on the condition, value, foreseeable problems, and necessary repairs that should be addressed.

After the inspection is complete, the home inspector will then present the buyer or client with a summary of these assessments, which is signed and can be notarized.

Before you choose an inspector, make sure you check their history, knowledge, reputation, and certifications. There are some professions in which you must be wary of scammers, and this unfortunately happens to be one of them. Most any person can say they are a home inspector, but do they have the experience to back the results? It pays to inquire.

Any "pro" home inspector will carry a state-sanctioned inspector's certification, which means he has been trained and licensed. He will also carry insurance and be a member of the National Association of Home Inspectors, which is a highly respected trade organization that ensures its members operate under a code of ethics. Currently, thirty-nine states require that home inspectors carry this certification. If they do not have it, then move on to another inspector who is more qualified. Believe me: Spending the money on a legitimate professional who carries a license can pay off greatly over time.

It's better to find out if your home of interest needs anything repaired prior to purchase rather than finding out a few months down the road that the whole roof needs to be replaced or that the home is filled with dangerous asbestos that could harm your family and pets!

REFERRALS MATTER! HOW TO FIND THE RIGHT HOME INSPECTOR

Ask your real estate agent for referrals, or family and friends who have recently purchased houses in the area. Here are some tips:

- If you are looking online, make sure the inspector has a legitimate website and professional presentation.

- Call and speak with at least two or three inspectors to compare notes about their rates, experience, and what they will deliver and how fast.

- Find out if the inspector is an accredited member of any professional organizations that serve the home inspection industry.

- Do they guarantee accuracy of the inspection and on the inspection report? What are the final document(s) they will prepare for you?

- Although fewer people check with the BBB (Better Business Bureau) these days, you can do this if you wish. It may behoove you to do a search online to find out if any complaints have ever been filed. Sometimes people also leave reviews.

- Ask questions! How many years have they been in

business? Does the inspector have any formal training to do home inspections? A qualified inspector has at least seven to ten years under their belt, and no, internet classes do not count as "formal training"!

• Don't forget to ask if your home inspector has errors and omissions insurance. This is a necessity in today's real estate industry, especially after the housing crisis. If something turns up that your inspector did not catch, they will be held legally liable.

Finally, consider where the referral for the home inspector came from. If it came from your Uncle Mike, who "knows a guy who has a next-door neighbor who does inspections," this may not be as good a referral as one given by your real estate agent, who deals with home inspections all the time.

EXACTLY WHAT DOES A HOME INSPECTION COVER?

Here are most of the things a home inspector will look at to determine if they are in good, working condition or in need of repairs:

• Kitchen and laundry appliances

• Bathrooms, vents, bath and shower

- Foundation or basement

- The building's framing, walls, and structure

- AC unit/heating system (hot and cool air units) furnace and vents

- Electrical wiring, fuse boxes, age of electrical system

- Non-cosmetic interior elements, like outlet covers and light fixtures

- Plumbing system

- Insulation

- Windows and doors

- Attic and chimney

- Roof

The inspector will be keeping an eye out for signs of dampness and mold as well as wood-destroying insects during the inspection. Some inspection companies also go the extra mile by testing for lead, radon, asbestos, carbon monoxide, and other hazardous toxins within the home.

In rural towns and municipalities where well water and septic systems are the norm, it is often required that buyers and/or sellers have special system flushings and inspections performed. Licensed pest-control inspectors are recommended to avoid the presence of commonly found carpenter ants and termites. A state-certified mold remediation company should be called should any dampness reveal evidence of mold. While your home inspector is not the one to perform these type of inspections, they may be a valuable resource in referring you to reputable companies who offer those sorts of services.

FAQS ABOUT INSPECTIONS

Here are eight of the most commonly asked questions about inspections:

FAQ #1: WHEN EXACTLY DOES A HOME INSPECTION TAKE PLACE?

The home inspection phase occurs during the "due diligence" period, after an offer has been accepted. After signing an accepted offer for a home, the clock starts ticking. Buyers standardly have anywhere from seven to fourteen days to get any inspections done and to negotiate repairs or a financial credit with the seller.

FAQ #2: HOW MUCH DOES AN INSPECTION COST?

In a real estate transaction, inspectors are hired by the homebuyer and can range from $300 to $600, depending on what services you request. In addition to a standard inspection, you can request testing for radon, carbon monoxide, and wood-eating insects. The more you request, the higher your inspection bill will be.

FAQ #3: HOW LONG DOES AN INSPECTION TAKE?

The inspection itself will take anywhere between two and five hours, depending on the size of the property, the length of time it takes to measure and take account of each room, and other factors. You should find out whether the home inspector charges a flat rate or an hourly fee, because if the person is a conversationalist and likes to stay and talk a lot while on the job, an hourly arrangement could be more costly than a fixed price.

FAQ #4: DO I NEED TO ATTEND THE INSPECTION?

The answer is a resounding *yes*! You should absolutely be there for the inspection. This is to ensure the inspection is done up to your expectations, as well as to make yourself available in case of questions.

Within a few days, the inspection report will be available.

Some inspectors can send the report to you on the same day. You may receive the report as a PDF that can be emailed to you, or you may choose to have it mailed or dropped off to you in person.

The benefit of having a report in hand is twofold. It offers you peace of mind that the residence of your choice is worth buying, and it's also a powerful negotiation tool. The inspection company provides the report on professional business stationery to make a good impression on the seller and their real estate firm.

FAQ #5: WHAT HAPPENS IF THE HOME FAILS INSPECTION?

Believe it or not, this happens a lot, and does not have to be the end of the world or the end of a deal. It is standard practice to request that the seller address anything that did not pass the inspection. Leaky roof, water penetration, mold in the basement, and rodent infestation are examples of a few negative marks that can show up on the report. It is within your right to ask that the seller fix them prior to purchase or to request a financial credit from the seller in order to have them repaired yourself after closing.

In your purchase agreement, you will likely find a section pertaining to your right to have a home inspection and also a right to waive this opportunity. This is a common clause on any real estate purchase and sales agreement. The agreement states that you will get a refund of your earnest money deposit if the home does not meet your approval upon inspection, should you decide to terminate the deal altogether.

FAQ #6: WHY WOULD ANYONE WANT TO SKIP A HOME INSPECTION?

The reasons buyers forgo the home inspection vary, from the over-zealous new buyer who adamantly gives the property a "once-over" with the naked eye, to the investor who feels using one of their own contractors is sufficient, to families who are already on a tight budget and want to save a little money on the closing costs. Too many people have learned the hard way that skipping a home inspection by a licensed inspector is always a *bad* idea! Don't forget about Mr. Know-It All.

That, my friends, is why I have devoted an entire chapter on this very topic! It is *that* important.

FAQ #7: WHAT IF OTHER BUYERS ARE MAKING AN OFFER ON THE PROPERTY AND THEY WAIVE THE INSPECTION CONTINGENCY?

If you feel that putting your foot down and asking for repairs will weaken your position with a seller who has multiple offers on the table, then bring a licensed contractor or handyman with you on a follow-up visit to check the home out prior to writing an offer. This way you can determine if the home is in good condition up front, then draft up an offer that is not contingent on inspection. Something like this should *only* be done for special circumstances when there is stiff competition.

FAQ #8: IS AN INSPECTION THE ONLY WAY I CAN GET HISTORY ABOUT A HOUSE?

Request that your real estate agent provide you with a full list of disclosures available on the home. Read them thoroughly. If there are multiple offers, you may need to consider whether an inspection contingency will hurt your chances (see FAQ #7). But if yours is the only offer on the table, you'll definitely want to go the full nine yards with inspection.

Find out up front the turnaround time for your inspection report. Make sure your inspector knows that time is critical, since you may not have a full day or even two to three days to put your offer in before someone else does. Some home inspectors can turn a report around within twenty-four hours, while others require at least three days. Usually, an inspector can tell you the condition of the home right then and there. If you must, you can base your decision to move forward from their verbal conclusions.

Again, don't let somebody sway you into thinking that a home inspection is not necessary. A friend, co-worker, or relative may say something like, "Oh, just go with your instincts." Or, "I didn't get an inspection when I bought my house and everything was fine. That's just extra money you'll have to spend, it's not worth it."

Tell them, "Thanks, but no thanks!" for their advice. Tell them about a story you read in my book about a guy who "knew it all" but ended up being stuck with a $20,000 repair bill for basement flooding and kitchen damage caused by faulty electrical issues . . . all of which could have been avoided if he would have just listened to his real estate agent.

CHAPTER 9

APPRAISALS:
Comps, Reports, Results
. . . Oh My!

YOU'VE FOUND THE HOME OF YOUR DREAMS AND they're asking $275,000. You already have an approval for that amount from your bank. But is the house really worth that amount? That's the question at the center of any home appraisal. The worth or value of the property will determine how much a lender is willing to give you to buy that particular piece of real estate.

Once you apply for your mortgage, the lender orders an appraisal of the home. This will usually occur right after your inspection is completed.

A home appraisal is a vital step in getting the financing you need to purchase, but a bad appraisal can kill the deal. The appraisal can also be a confusing part of the home-buying process in which both buyer and seller must depend on the expert opinion of an outsider. A real estate appraisal is simply that—the expert opinion of a certified, state-licensed professional who determines the value of a piece of property. If your $500,000 dream home is really worth only $430,000, then the home is overpriced.

A home appraisal also protects your mortgage company from getting stuck with a property that's worth less than they've loaned to the borrower on a mortgage. Look at it this way: It protects you from paying too much for a house simply because it was love at first sight. The home appraisal is a no-nonsense factor in a decision that is often emotional for the buyer.

APPRAISAL METHODS

When you apply for a mortgage, your lender typically requires the property be appraised by one of their approved licensed appraisers. This practice helps create more consistent appraisals and gives you assurance that the appraiser is properly credentialed and that their findings are held in the highest regard by your mortgage lender. Even though the home appraisal is the lender's requirement, it is the borrower's responsibility. You usually pay for it as part of the financing costs at the time of closing. The cost is typically around $300 (give or take a few dollars) depending on the size of the property.

There are two primary appraisal methods for residential

property. In the *sales-comparison approach*, the appraiser compares the property with four or five similar homes that have sold in the area, often called comparables, or "comps." This method is very similar to what your real estate agent does during comparative market analysis, the difference being that a comparative market analysis is more informal. An appraisal considers specific components, such as lot size, square footage of finished and unfinished space, style and age of house, as well as other features, such as garages and fireplaces.

The *cost approach* to appraisal is used more often for new property and is based on reproduction costs. The appraiser estimates the cost to replace the structure if it were to be destroyed. The appraiser then looks at land value and depreciation to determine the property's total worth.

The appraiser gathers information for the appraisal report from a number of sources, but the process often begins with a physical inspection of the property inside and out. This is a less in-depth assessment than the home inspector's, but it is no less important. Additionally, the appraiser may look at county courthouse records and recent reports from the local real estate multiple listing services. The difference between a real estate agent doing a CMA and a licensed appraiser doing a full appraisal is the level of science, analysis, and detail that go into the appraiser's methodology.

WHAT DOES THE APPRAISAL REPORT INCLUDE?

The appraisal report generally includes:

- A comparative market analysis that supports the appraisal

- The size and condition of the house and other permanent fixtures, along with a description of any improvements that have been made and the materials used

- An explanation of how the appraiser determined the value of the property

- Statements regarding serious structural problems, such as a damp basement or cracked foundation

- Notes about the surrounding area or community

- An evaluation of recent market trends in the area that may affect the value

- Maps and photographs

Keep in mind that the appraisal amount is not only for the house itself. In fact, the figure considers the total value of the home, any other structural upgrades and permanent fixtures, along with the land that the house is built on.

THREE THINGS TO KNOW IF THE APPRAISAL COMES IN TOO LOW

Imagine that you learn that your dream home is only valued at $249,000—a full $26,000 lower than the asking price! If you are the buyer, this figure means that the amount you can finance the property for is much lower than you expected, because the lender will only loan up to the appraised amount. And you already have an accepted offer! An appraised value that is considerably lower than what you have offered should be a red light—a warning that you may be paying too much. So is the deal over? Is it time to panic and throw in the towel?

First, I'd recommend taking a look at what may have caused the low appraisal. It might be due to factors that the homeowner could correct, such as repairs or maintenance. If that's the case, the appraiser may be willing to take a second look and adjust the appraisal accordingly.

Second, you always have the option to order a second appraisal. This may be a good idea if the first appraiser is inexperienced or unfamiliar with the area where the property is located. It's possible that a second appraisal will uncover mistakes the first appraiser made. If you believe that an appraisal is simply not an accurate representation of the property's value, and the appraiser is not willing to listen to your concerns, you can go to your state licensing agency for appraisers and file a complaint.

So, what happens when you've exhausted both of those options? Your lender won't loan more than the appraisal. So what do you do? Here are three options:

1. Have your attorney or agent go back to the sellers with the new appraisal. Perhaps the seller will lower the asking price or carry a second mortgage to make up the difference. After all, if the house won't appraise well for you, nine times out of ten it won't appraise well for anyone.

2. Pay the difference between the selling price and appraisal price out of pocket. Although it's not my favorite option, if the buyers love the house and they know they'll be in it long enough to see the value rise, then this becomes a viable option. To determine if this option makes sense, consider what the difference in price is.

3. Lastly, if negotiations fall through and the appraisal is still too far below what the bank is willing to finance, then there is no other choice than to cancel the transaction. Walk away

and don't look back! You've done all you can do. You probably signed a purchasing contract stating your offer for the property, but if your agent has advised you well, it will have contained an appraisal contingency and a loan contingency, each of which may give you an "out" should certain conditions not be met. This is a statement that allows you to cancel the contract and receive any deposit you paid the seller if you don't qualify to buy the property at the agreed terms.

With those things in mind, let the appraiser do his job. Questions and banter may make the inspection go slowly or make the appraiser miss something. It is wise to take your own set of notes while the appraiser assessing. Then, when he is done, feel free to ask any questions you may have.

Now that we've gotten a thorough understanding of "Appraisals 101," let's move onto the traps and catch-22s I want to save *every* homebuyer the headache of ever having to experience! Are you still with me? Good! Strap on your seatbelt, and let's go!

CHAPTER 10

COMMON PITFALLS TO AVOID:
Home Buying No-No's

PURCHASING A HOUSE FOR THE FIRST-TIME, OR EVEN the second, third, or fourth time can be a great experience. Or it can be a nightmare, if you don't avoid some of the common mistakes unwary buyers often make. Of course, my goal in writing this book is so you will have a pleasant and memorable experience in purchasing your first property, and end up with a home you love.

I once worked with a Property Virgin that I called *Tweet*. It was a funny nickname I gave her after working together for two weeks. Each time she saw a home feature that she loved, she would jump up and down and make a high-pitched chirp like a bird. No, I'm not joking! Her mother was assisting her in the search and informed me that she had been "tweeting or chirping" since childhood . . . LOL.

As I drove to meet her at what would later be called her "dream home," the seller's agent called to advise me that the homeowner would be there while we toured. It's never a good idea to tour a home with the homeowner looking over your shoulder and listening intently to client feedback. But since we were already on our way, there was really nothing that could be done. As we walked up to the front door, I advised Tweet to try and contain her emotion because the seller would be present. If we decided to make an offer later on, we'd want to maintain our poker face to keep the upper hand.

As we walked through the foyer into the great room, I noticed a huge smile come over my client's face. The good news was that she loved it. The bad news was that the seller knew it. We continued into the kitchen and dining room, and the tweeting started. "Oh my goodness, this is it! I can't believe we're standing in my kitchen," she proclaimed. Uh oh. The seller stood in the entryway and heard the entire proclamation. I asked the seller if she could give us a little privacy as we toured the rest of the home, and as she obliged, I virtually shook the tweets out of Tweet. Unfortunately, it was too late.

Later that evening, we put in an offer on the house for $435,000. Considering the property was listed for $449,000 and had been on the market for forty-two days without another offer, it was a fair entry proposal. Wouldn't you know it; the seller got cocky and wouldn't budge. She refused to come down one dollar. Tweet was stunned to find out the seller wanted full asking price and wasn't willing to negotiate. I suggested she sit on her offer for a week or two to let the seller get nervous. But Tweet was adamant that she didn't want to lose her "dream house" and didn't want to take any chances. Sadly, she wound up paying full asking price, all because she couldn't contain her emotions.

This leads me into the common pitfalls to avoid when purchasing a house.

NINE WAYS TO RUIN THE JOY OF BUYING A HOUSE

Have you ever seen the movie, *How to Lose a Guy in Ten Days?* It features the lovely Kate Hudson doing everything in her power to "mess up" her relationship with a guy (Matthew McConaughey), all for the sake of an article she is writing for a magazine.

Just like relationships, you can unknowingly ruin the joy of buying property. It can be quite a rush to buy your own house, especially if this is the first time for you. You may be so overjoyed that you can mess up the negotiating side, or forgo the inspection, or forget something really, really important on your contract that, down the road, you will wish had been there. These are all good reasons to solidify my advice of choosing professionals to work with you. If you have a team in place, the process should be rather pleasant. If not, it can be downright nightmarish.

AVOID THESE NINE HOME-BUYING NO-NO'S:

1. **Being Overly Enthusiastic**: You must be able to manage your emotions. You have to show your "poker face" sometimes, at least in the presence of the seller. When you speak with your real estate broker, though, you should be honest about your feelings. As an agent myself, I much prefer clients who tell me openly about any concerns they might have, rather than waiting until the last minute. It is our job to find you the right home that fits your needs and that you will love to live in. Most realtors will bend over backward to do that for you, but if you have any excitement or glee that you want to express in front of the seller, I would encourage you to curb your enthusiasm.

   It is great to be genuinely interested, but if they know you really want the place, it could make them hold on the price instead of being flexible—just like in Tweet's situation. Trust me; it is difficult to deal with rigid sellers!

2. **Failing to Consider the Resale Value**: People who buy a home for the first-time often think they will live in it forever, but the reality is that on average, people only live in their first two homes for seven to ten years. Circumstances change and life happens, so it's vital to consider the resale value in any decision you make on a home. Perhaps you don't mind living three houses down from a liquor store. But chances are another buyer will when it's time to sell. Perhaps painting the house lime green seems like a joyous

idea. But how many people do you suppose will want to live in a house the color of a Popsicle? Not many. By all means, enjoy the quality of your home to the utmost while you're living there. However, when it comes time to put that same house back on the market, be prepared to give it an overhaul. This is of course if you'd like to get top market dollar when it sells.

3. **Living Outside of Your Financial Comfort Zone:** Another error homebuyers tend to make is getting caught up in living outside of their financial means. This can be one of your biggest heartaches and regrets. The joys of homeownership can become your worst nightmare if you make mistakes with the budget. Some buyers get dazzled by a particular home and so they start thinking, "Well, it's a little more than I planned on spending, but I'll work extra hours to make up the difference." Or, "I should be getting a raise soon, so I will be able to afford it." This kind of thinking can get you in a lot of hot water! It happens all too often: unforeseen circumstances arise that instantly change a family's income level. No one can predict job loss, death in the family, lawsuits, or IRS debts. And then there are the planned challenges such as adding another child to the family or paying for college tuition. All of these can drastically change your monthly bottom line.

You want to enjoy life, and not be stuck in survival mode. I've seen many families who end up cutting themselves short, especially if unexpected expenses arise and leave them in a pinch. If your car breaks down, for example, and the repairman tells you that it's a $600 job, will that hinder your ability to pay your mortgage for the month? It is better to make a purchase that is completely manageable from the beginning. Then, when financial tornadoes come your way, they won't wipe you out.

I prefer to tell people that their mortgage payment should be equivalent to about one week's salary, or a quarter of your take-home pay (post-taxes) to be on the safe side. By choosing a house that is affordable, you can enjoy being there more! People who are "house poor" often have to work long, long hours to make up the difference of having a more expensive house, thereby spending less time at home living in it and instead "working to live and living to work." I don't know about you, but I'd rather be home digging in my flower garden or playing with my daughter in the backyard on the weekends instead of working two or three jobs just to cover my mortgage. Wouldn't you agree?

4. **Not Having An Emergency Fund:** Keep in mind that with homeownership also comes unexpected expenses. If something breaks, you will shell out the money to fix it, unlike having a landlord. It's best to have a contingency account for those "just in case" scenarios that can happen to anyone.

One idea I came up with to help people save for for these occasions is to use a Holiday Club savings program. What's a Holiday Club? Banks often have savings programs to help customers save up for presents, and this is a similar idea. But there are other neat things about it. For one, it is barely noticeable when you save $10 or $20 per week out of your paycheck; whereas, if you were to add that up and try to come up with that much out of the blue, it could set you back. CDs, mutual funds, and money market accounts are another good option, but only if you are willing to put in a substantial lump sum to open the account. In contrast, the Holiday Club is the same amount each week (usually $5, $10, $20, etc.). These smaller amounts can be easier to manage and will pay off if you get in a jam with a surprise house repair.

5. **Shopping for a Home Before Speaking with the Bank:** This falls in line with my prequalification and preapproval advice. Some misguided people start looking at homes with their real estate agent before speaking to the bank. This can present a real snag in the home-buying process and can drag it out for weeks! There's nothing like spending months searching for the right house in your perceived $350,000 range. Then you finally find and make an offer, only to get turned down by the bank when they say you should have been looking for a $250,000 house instead of a $350,000 house. *Ouch!*

6. **Forgetting to Save for Furnishings and Other Necessities:** After draining your bank account to put money down on the house, it can be rather annoying to move in and have *nothing* to sit or sleep on. Rather than racking up the credit

cards at a furniture store, plan to save enough in addition to your down payment to buy the essentials. Don't forget about things you will need to maintain your home, like a lawn mower or ladder, if you don't already own these things. Stash some money on the side to purchase what you need. This should be separate from your "rainy day" account, which should have six months of living expenses in it.

7. **Buying a Big Item Prior to Closing:** I've seen it happen. A couple does all of the right things, including getting pre-approved, shopping for a house with an agent, and making sure the home passes inspection. Then, while waiting to close on their home, they run out and purchase three rooms of furniture on credit. This is a no-no! Banks approve you for your mortgage based upon your credit score and savings at the time of approval. Your approval is contingent upon those items remaining the same through closing. If you run up a $5,000 line of credit at a furniture store, your credit score immediately changes. Banks check borrowers' credit several times before the closing contracts are signed. If your mortgage company sees any major changes in your credit, they may decline the loan or change the terms of the loan. It's best not to take any chances and just be patient on any big purchases.

8. **Buying Too Young:** Young people often have more chances of moving, for a career change, for love, and many other reasons. When you're in your early twenties, you may feel like

this is a place you'll want to live forever, but by the next year some major life event could change your plans. Please wait until you are stable before making such a huge commitment. I don't mean to dissuade any youngsters from buying. Afterall, I purchased my first property in my early twenties. But it's important to be mindful of this.

9. **Buying a house with a boyfriend or girlfriend**: Before I tell you a story, let me just say that your love may not last as long as your relationship with the mortgage company, especially if you are still getting to know someone. I have even seen couples who have been together a long time—from seven to ten years—commit to buying a house jointly, but then things went awry. It can be complicated to get someone else's name off the mortgage and deed of the property. If you want to live together, then I would recommend whomever in the relationship has the best credit should make the purchase of the home solely in his or her name, to avoid the hassle of a potentially sticky situation.

I've had at least nine clients that I can think of off the top of my head experience the ugly truth of these common mistakes. The one who best illustrates my point was a twenty-eight-year-old IT manager. When Geoff was referred to me, the poor guy was balding from stress. He'd been with his girlfriend, Laura, since college, and they both assumed they'd get married one day, so they decided to purchase a house first. After only a year of living in the home together, he fell in love with a coworker and decided to break it off with his college sweetheart. Little did he know she wasn't going to be swept aside easily.

Although Geoff was paying the bulk of the bills, the home was in both of their names and Laura refused to move out. In her eyes, he should be the one to move since he broke it off. Problem was, his down payment was tied up in the house. And he knew she couldn't afford to pay the mortgage on the house herself if he left. He broke her heart, and it was clear she was planning to break his pockets.

Geoff decided to put the house on the market and try to sell and get out clean. Whenever a buyer would come by for a home tour, Laura refused to let them in, telling them, "This house isn't for sale!" Finally, after five months of being stuck in the house together, Jeff got an offer. Laura refused to sign the deal unless he gave her $40,000 cash. Now, that's what you call an ugly break-up!

Much like most lessons we learn in life, experience is the best teacher. So I could tell you chapter and verse every single possible mistake to avoid, and some things simply won't register until you actually go through the process yourself. My goal in this section was to give you options and show you how you could save yourself time, money, and headaches. Our instincts are often right, so remember my "no-no" advice, listen to your inner voice, and ultimately *go with your gut*!

CHAPTER 11

THE TITLE
SCRUB DOWN:

Not All Title Companies
Are Created Equal

YOU MAY REMEMBER THAT IN CHAPTER 7 WE TOUCHED upon the possibility of using a real estate attorney to oversee the closing or "settlement" process. Another option is to hire a title company. The cornerstone of this phase of the real estate purchase transaction is filing or recording the deed or title to the property with the local municipality in which you are buying. Once submitted and registered, this document makes the home officially yours.

Most people are quite bewildered when it comes to the title and obtaining title insurance. What is it? What is the purpose?

UNDERSTANDING TITLES

Essentially, a title company's sole purpose is to ensure that a property title is clean and legitimate—that is, that the individual is indeed the rightful owner of both the land and its buildings. Imagine back in the old days of horses and wagons riding through the prairie, their occupants ready to stake their claim to any parcel of land they wanted. These homesteaders pitched a sign into the ground with their name on it and said, "This is my land!"

These days, of course, things are done much differently. Because that land has passed through so many hands, and so many generations of people have now owned that once "raw" piece of land, we now have title companies in place to verify the rightful ownership of a given property.

The process starts with a title search, which is performed through a thorough examination of the records to ensure that the person claiming to own the property is in fact the person who is selling it. You don't want to give your hard-earned money to just anyone who says, "This is my house."

If this sounds ridiculous, believe me, it's not! Sometimes, through careful and meticulous scouring through property records, you might find an error. Someone may have died and left their estate to one or several heirs, and now perhaps one of those heirs is selling it without telling the other relatives. Or perhaps the home was involved in some kind of a legal dispute, such as a divorce or bankruptcy. As strange as it may seem, this is more common than you realize!

That's the reason a title company is necessary. The title company will research everything having to do with the property before the closing, including any outstanding liens, back debts, unpaid taxes, legally registered owners, and more. The title company also digs deeper to find out if there are any leases—such as renters who are currently living in the home—and other restrictions or easements that might affect your ability to take over ownership. These issues must be addressed before the closing. When a title company finds problems, it can delay the process of closing until the issues are resolved.

In most cases, the title company requests a property survey to clarify the exact boundaries of the stated plot of land. This is especially important in cases where fences may have been put up that go "over the line," or on properties in which the acreage is more than just a specified allotment within a subdivision. Good fences make good neighbors, right? Well, it would be no fun for you to move into your new house and suddenly discover that your neighbors own half of your backyard, or that they are infringing upon your space. This isn't the best way to begin a relationship with your neighbors. Not to worry, though, the title company will clear up any such hassles.

While we're on that note, the title company has another important job, and that is to maintain the escrow. The escrow is the "holding" account for your deposit so that the money is ready to be given to the seller on the day of closing. It is also common for real estate brokerages or real estate attorneys to hold checks in escrow for you. You can't just give a blank check to your real estate broker or your lawyer; it has to be filled out with the intent that it will be held on your behalf. This is to ensure that your money is held for safekeeping until the closing.

At closing, the money held in escrow will be distributed to the appropriate parties. Checks will be cut for the seller, the real estate broker, the attorney, and all of the other parties who are expecting to get paid. If it's hard to part with those fees, don't feel too bad! You are just about to embark upon a new chapter in your life: homeownership.

CHOOSING A TITLE COMPANY

To give you greater peace of mind, here are some questions to ask the title company before you choose who to hire:

- How long have you been in business?

- Are you local, or do you serve other regions, too?

- Do you disclose the findings (also known as "exceptions")?

- How do you protect money in escrow, and how safe is it?

- Who performs the title research? Is it done individually or by an outside party?

- Do you have any conflicts of interest, such as a contractor or mortgage company that also owns a title agency?

- What are your rates?

- How long does the title search and delivery processes take, as well as any other surveys that might be part of it?

WHY TITLE INSURANCE IS NECESSARY

Title insurance is another aspect of your home-buying experience. What is title insurance for, exactly? It's not just another way to get you to spend your hard-earned dollars; title insurance protects the bank and the owner of the house against any lawsuits that might occur due to title discrepancies or disputes.

There are two different kinds of title insurance. One is the owner's title insurance, which keeps the owner out of hot water in case any problems are found during the discovery process. The second is lender's title insurance, which protects the lender. Your mortgage company wants to ensure their money is in good hands.

More than likely, your home will be your biggest investment, and title insurance protects your interest in that investment. Title insurance protects real estate owners and lenders against any property loss or damage they might experience because of liens, encumbrances, or defects in the title to the property. Without title insurance, you may not be fully protected against errors in public records. As a result, you may be held fully accountable for any prior claims brought against your new property. If this should occur, your title policy insures that you will be defended at no cost against all covered claims up to the amount of the policy.

Each title insurance policy is subject to specific terms, conditions, and exclusions. Title insurance is different from other types of insurance in that it protects you, the insured, from a loss that may occur from matters or faults from the past. Other types of insurance, such as auto, life, or health, cover you against losses that may occur in the future. Title insurance does not protect you against future faults, but it does protect you from undiscovered interests. Another difference is that you pay a one-time premium for a policy that remains effective until the property is sold to a new owner.

Title insurance is issued after a careful examination of the public records. But even the most thorough search cannot absolutely ensure that no title faults are present, despite the knowledge and experience of professional title examiners. In addition to matters shown by public records, other title problems may exist that cannot be disclosed in a search. Title insurance eliminates any risks and losses caused by faults in title from an event that occurred before you owned the property.

Real estate brokers (at least the best ones) will often try to refer the best title companies they prefer. However, the selection is ultimately the decision of the homebuyer, and the responsibility lies completely on their shoulders. This holds true for title insurance, as well. You don't have to stick to the names given if you want to do some additional shopping around for better rates. It's totally up to you.

FAQS ABOUT TITLE INSURANCE

Here are some of the most commonly asked questions about title insurance.

FAQ #1: WHAT MISHAPS CAN TITLE INSURANCE PROTECT YOU FROM?

- Improperly recorded legal documents

- Undisclosed heirs

- Gaps in the chain of title

- False impersonation of the true landowner

- Inadequate legal descriptions

- Conveyances by undisclosed divorced spouses

- Forged deeds, mortgages, and wills

- Documents executed under false, revoked, or expired powers of attorney

- State inheritance and gift tax liens

- Errors in tax records

- Failure to include necessary parties to certain judicial proceedings

- Improper or expired notarization

- Deeds by minors

- Issues of rightful possession of the land

- Deeds and mortgages by foreigners who may lack legal capacity to hold title

- Issues involving improper marital status

- Conveyances in violation of public policy

- Special tax assessments

- Forfeitures of property due to criminal acts

- Payment of legal costs if the title insurer has to defend your title against a covered claim

- Payment of successful claims against the title to your home covered by the policy, up to the cost of the policy

FAQ #2: WHAT COULD HAPPEN IF YOU SKIP TITLE INSURANCE?

There have been criminal cases where a seller has knowingly tried to sell a home he or she doesn't own. Or instances of renters posing as sellers. But more often than not, problems with titles happen because a seller simply does not know any better. The seller might have co-purchased the house ten years ago with a girlfriend or boyfriend they haven't talked to in years and are unaware that they need the other person's signature to sell. Or the seller might have inherited the house under the terms of a will that turned out to have been out-of-date and a more recent will leaves the house to someone else. These things happen all the time!

I remember a story involving a newly divorced mother who had just landed her first job in eight years after being a stay-at-home mom. She decided to buy her first home on her own in New Jersey. Money was limited, so she decided to cut a few corners.

She learned that the title company was going to conduct a full search of the bankruptcy courts, and land and court records so she figured she could save a few hundred dollars by not buying a title insurance policy.

At the closing table, the single mother met the seller, a nice, older gentleman named Mr. J, who had lived in the house for fifteen years. About three months after the settlement, the mother's eldest son answered the front door. He was greeted by a woman who asked, "Who are you, and why are you in my house?" The woman produced her driver's license, which identified her as Mrs. J. The home address of the property was listed below her name.

Apparently Mr. & Mrs. J had purchased and lived in the home together up until their divorce. She had kept her last name and relocated to Philadelphia to live with her sister. Upon divorcing, they agreed that Mr. J would stay in the home and cover all expenses attached to the home while living there. But in the event the home was to be sold, both parties were to have split the proceeds. Nothing was ever recorded in the Recorder of Deeds Office in New Jersey, and because the divorce proceedings happened in Philadelphia, nothing showed up when the title company searched the New Jersey court records.

Research revealed that Mr. J had forged the ex-wife's signature on the listing agreement, and the power of attorney. To make matters worse, Mrs. J and the single mother learned that Mr. J had the net sales proceeds wired to an offshore bank account and had apparently moved out of the country and vanished.

So where does this leave the single mother? Well, it wasn't pretty. A forged deed cannot convey a clear title to the purchaser.

So when Mr. J signed the deed, he only signed over his fifty percent interest. Consequently, the single mom did not have clear title to one hundred percent of the home. Mrs. J, never having signed the deed, still owned her half of the home. Had the single mother purchased owner's title insurance, she could have simply filed a title claim, and the title insurance company would have hired attorneys, at their expense, to sort out the mess.

FAQ #3: HOW MUCH WILL TITLE INSURANCE COST?

Homebuyers don't tend to pay much attention to the title insurance required by their mortgage lender, that is, until they see the charge on their list of closing costs. Title insurance rates vary considerably state to state and can run anywhere from a few hundred dollars to a few thousand. The insurance commission approves and controls the premiums for title insurance policies. Premiums are paid only once, and the cost depends upon the purchase price of the property. The policy amount must be equal to the purchase price. But considering all the coverage noted above, it's a bargain in the end.

If you examine the cost of title insurance over the life of the policy versus other types of insurance, you'll find that it's a great value for the money spent. It has been estimated that if a homeowner were to pay the national average cost of a title insurance policy and live in their home for just five years, the annual average cost of the title insurance policy would be less than $200 a year. Compare that with the annual cost of a homeowners policy, which can range from $500 to $2,500 per year, depending on the replacement cost of a home.

Many homebuyers rely on their mortgage broker or real estate agent to select a title agent. But take it from me, you are better off making the selection yourself. I recommend asking your real estate lawyer to recommend an independent title company, and to avoid title agencies that have a business affiliation with any real estate agency or lender recommending them.

CHAPTER 12

THE CLOSING TABLE:
The Final Frontier

AWESOME! IF YOU'VE MADE IT OVER MOST OF THE hurdles and taken the advice I've given you thus far, then perhaps you will find yourself sitting with your real estate agent and real estate attorney at the closing table.

It can be nerve-wracking, yet exciting when you are presented with a big contract in which you will be required to "sign your life away." But really, this is where your new life as a homeowner begins. You should be thrilled that you finally made it to the table. I hope you're smiling from ear to ear!

But wait; there are a few more things we must address before you sign on the dotted lines. In this chapter, we will talk about homeowners insurance, private mortgage insurance, and how to prepare and exactly what to expect at the closing table. Ugh.

Doesn't sound like much fun, I know. Nevertheless, these are things you will have to sew up in order to close on your new house.

One way to ensure all is going as planned is to tell the lender that you want to review the documents before closing. You should also ask your attorney to do so. A lot of people fail to do this, and when they get to closing, they are embarrassed to ask questions and try to rush through the paperwork. That's when trouble comes in. You should understand every single document you will be signing upfront.

By law, you have the right to review the closing settlement statement, or the HUD-1 form, at least twenty-four hours before closing. Compare that form to the good faith estimate you received when you applied for the loan. It is also standard that you will be allowed a final walk-through inspection twenty-four hours before closing to determine if any damage was done to the property between contract and closing, and to negotiate any necessary repairs with the seller.

It is important for you to bring to the closing table every document received throughout the home-buying process. These include the good faith estimate and proof of homeowners insurance. It is also wise to bring a copy of your original purchase contract and inspection, just in case you need to refer to it for any reason.

Don't forget to bring a bank check for the amount you were stated. Many buyers are so anxious on closing day that they forget they need to stop at the bank to get the check. Get the check at least a day or two in advance. The other most important thing a homebuyer can bring to the closing table is patience! Closings usually take one to three hours and that's on a standard closing with no hiccups. I've been to closings that have lasted the greater part of a day. This is definitely something you don't want to try and schedule during a lunch break.

Another important piece of advice: Expect the unexpected! Human error is common, and one of the biggest delays in closings tends to be errors on the mortgage documents. Imagine you were approved for an interest rate of 3.25 percent but the mortgage docs say 4.98 percent. Would you feel comfortable signing it? Absolutely not! The changes will have to be made by the mortgage company before the closing can continue. Delays, delays, delays.

This kind of situation is why I reiterate reading *everything* in great detail ahead of time. If a document doesn't look familiar, take your time and ask questions. You want to know what you're signing!

I also recommend trying to schedule your closing sometime around the end of the month, but *not* on the last day of the month. The last day of the month is the day most often requested for closing because the closer you are to the end of the month, the less closing costs tend to be. That's because prepaid interest due at closing accumulates throughout the month, but can be avoided or reduced if the closing is near the end of the month.

What if something goes wrong and you aren't able to close that day? What if closing lasts until evening and the mortgage company closes before you're finished? What if there is a computer error or the fax or printer is on the fritz? I'll tell you what happens: Everything gets pushed to the top of the next month and then your closing costs are increased due to taxes and interest for a full month, versus a pro-rated month being due. So it's in your best interest to review the documents ahead of time and catch any errors before they get to the table.

WHO WILL BE AT CLOSING?

- You

- Your agent

- Home seller

- Seller's real estate agent

- Title company representative

- Transaction attorney or attorneys for both sides

- Closing agent. This person conducts the meeting and makes sure all documents are signed and the fees and escrow payments paid.

THE LOWDOWN ON HOMEOWNERS INSURANCE

One of the itemized expenses you may see on your closing documents is a line item for homeowners insurance. Each state does things a little differently. In some states you are expected to buy homeowners insurance independently and then provide your attorney and the mortgage company with an annual record of payment. In other states you are expected to pay your annual homeowners insurance at the closing table. Then your mortgage company will bill you for it and make the payments on your behalf.

This is similar to when you purchase a car and have a car loan; the bank requires that you carry full coverage automobile insurance as long as you still have a lien on the car. Even past that point, most states now require car insurance for every registered vehicle. In the same way, you must have proof of homeowners insurance in place when you obtain a mortgage from any lender or else they will not secure the loan. If you buy your house outright, this is not mandatory, but anyone with a sound mind who cares about their property will of course want to have it insured!

CHILL PILL #22

When it comes to choosing homeowners insurance policies, always shop around for the best coverage, not the best price. This is one area in which being cheap or cutting corners will not yield any rewards.

Be smart, though, and do some price-comparison shopping. Not just any old homeowners insurance will do, no sir-ee. The cheap ones usually cover only basic things, and often put you through a lot of red tape when you need to file a claim to get reimbursed for loss or damages. Don't forget my story about "Mr. Know-It-All," the client who went against my advice on the home inspection and then ended up with about $20,000 of repair costs. Although he did have homeowners insurance, if you were in a similar situation and had barely any coverage, then most likely there would be higher deductibles and out-of-pocket costs.

Much like car insurance, which is required before you can even drive a vehicle off the sales lot, a home must be insured with at least enough liability and hazard coverage to cover replacement costs for the property. If, God forbid, the home burns down and it is under-insured or even worse, uninsured, your mortgage company can and most likely *will* come after to you to pay back the loan—even though you no longer have a house to live in.

To get the best coverage and price, you should get at least three quotes. There are a couple of ways to go about this. If you go online, you will likely find thousands of choices within your state and region. Call and speak with a live person or visit three well-established and reputable insurance companies in person. If you like your car insurance provider and have a good rapport, ask if they offer homeowners insurance. They may even offer a discount for opening an additional policy. You could also ask the lender that you plan on using whom they like working with or find most dependable. Your realtor might also have some advice, since he or she is most likely well-connected to other professionals in the industry.

After you decide which type of coverage you need, you can try to get the insurance company to agree to a lower rate. This is another area that is negotiable, since there are so many consumer options available to savvy homebuyers. Make sure you add on hazard insurance if you live in areas that are susceptible to catastrophic weather conditions, such as hurricanes, tornadoes, or flooding.

HOW YOUR CREDIT SCORE AFFECTS YOUR HOMEOWNERS INSURANCE RATE

Although we spoke in greater detail about your credit score in Chapter 6, while we're on the topic of homeowners insurance, it seems worth another mention. Did you know that your credit score has an impact on the price you will pay for homeowners insurance? Even though having homeowners insurance is mandatory for any real estate purchase these days, the price can be greater or lesser depending on your credit score. Although this sounds unfair, insurance companies use a similar mindset to mortgage lenders in that they want to protect their investment. Studies have revealed that people with lower credit scores are riskier customers than people who have higher scores.

You see, homeowners insurance companies are in the business of risk. They try to estimate how many claims their customers will file each year. Typically, those who are less financially responsible or who have lower scores are more likely to file a claim. Individual insurance companies have created their own rating numbers for customers based on their credit scores. Those with high scores are offered better rates; whereas, those with lower scores can expect to pay more.

So the million-dollar question is, what can you do to get better rates? Start by asking the insurance company what kind of scoring system they use. Then, ask if you qualify for the best rates and terms. If not, find out what you can do to qualify for them. Typically, anything that improves your credit score will also improve your insurance costs. You can also score discounts for having a home security system, paying the entire premium up front, paying by automatic billing, or purchasing your car insurance and homeowners insurance from the same company. Shopping around can ensure that you find the best available price, no matter what your credit score.

CHILL PILL #23

Get every discount available to you when you choose home insurance. You may be able to pay a lower premium because you also have car insurance with the same carrier or because the home you are purchasing has a security system already installed. However, don't sacrifice obtaining the maximum coverage that fits within your budget, because accepting lower coverage could leave you having to pay out-of-pocket expenses in the event of a claim for damage or loss. With so many options available to homebuyers, insurance companies are in a position to negotiate. Some people just settle for the price they are quoted without realizing they could have "haggled" on price! Every bit you can save on your monthly mortgage payment adds up to bigger savings at the end of the year.

DON'T PMS ABOUT PMI: UNDERSTANDING PRIVATE MORTGAGE INSURANCE

Let's move onto the other line items you may find itemized on your closing statement, such as private mortgage insurance, or PMI. To recap once more, PMI is an insurance policy that lenders require buyers to purchase if their down payment is less than 20 percent. PMI covers the lender, not the homeowner, for up to 20 percent of the home price if the homeowner defaults and goes into foreclosure. Buyers are required to pay for this insurance until the loan-to-value ratio reaches 80 percent.

So for instance, if you are purchasing a home for $200,000, and it appraises for that exact amount, you would have to hand over a down payment of no less than $40,000 (20 percent cash equity) and take a mortgage of no more than $160,000 to avoid being required to pay PMI.

Before considering this to be an ideal alternative to saving up for a large down payment, keep in mind that PMI premiums can be costly. They may run between half a percent to one percent of the mortgage total amount each year. That can translate to several thousands of dollars per year. Insurance premiums are an extra cost and are not applied to the mortgage balance.

When you are considering your budget and how much your mortgage payment will be, be aware of these extra fees that can add up on top of your monthly payment and cause unforeseen setbacks. The object here is to enjoy life in your new home, not to be scraping by financially.

CHAPTER 13

UNLOCKING THE DOORS TO YOUR NEW HOME:
Now What?

WHEW! **AFTER YOU GET UP FROM THE CLOSING** table and shake hands with all of the parties who are present, it might be tempting to jump up and down or do a little dance. It's like hitting a home run or scoring a touchdown, except now you are officially a new homeowner! You should have a profound sense of freedom and relief.

I often feel like jumping up and down with my clients, because I get so close to them throughout the process. I learn about their families, and we develop a personal connection. It's a great feeling for me, too, when I see a couple or family who has finally reached their dream of homeownership.

When the seller finally hands over the keys to your new home, it can feel surreal. It is a much more rewarding experience than getting the keys to a rental apartment or any place you've lived before. Now you have a place that is truly yours! It is not just a house; it is a home.

Owning a home can represent many different things. For some people, it may mean stability for their family. For others, it may provide financial security, since mortgage payments are often significantly less than what you pay in rent.

However, just because you finally have the keys in your hand, the transaction is not entirely finished. Sure, you can do your happy dance if you like! You've earned it. Then, after you are done dancing around the living room and buying new plants and homey decorations and making a list of whom to invite to your housewarming party, remember to do the following twenty-one things.

What?! The work's not over yet? No, not quite. Smart buyers take the time to prepare their home before move-in and to learn all the nuances of their property. Even a brand-new home in move-in condition will require upkeep. Completing this brief checklist within the first two weeks of your closing date will give you greater peace of mind that you have done everything in your power to make homeownership a joyful and pleasant experience.

Rest easy. I promise this list is easier than what you've just been through finding and purchasing your new home!

THINGS TO DO AFTER YOU TAKE
OVER OWNERSHIP OF YOUR NEW PLACE:

1. Call to make utility bill transfers.

2. Change the locks on the doors.

3. Make sure the latches and locks on all the windows are functioning correctly.

4. Set up home security, if necessary.

5. Call pest control and have your new house treated, both interior and exterior to just to be safe against termites and rodents.

6. Look for local landscapers if you are not in an HOA community that covers it.

7. Find a handyman who can help you with small repairs around the house.

8. Change the air filters (and continue to do so monthly or bi-monthly).

9. Get the dryer vents cleaned to avoid a fire.

10. Check the date the hot water heater was last bled.

11. Give the house another deep cleaning; you can never be too sure even if it "looks" clean or is "broom clean."

12. Get moved in.

13. Unpack your boxes.

14. Drive around and learn shortcuts and discover where things like the nearest grocery store and gas station are located.

15. Get blinds and curtains.

16. Introduce your family to the neighbors.

17. Two weeks after closing, contact local municipalities to make sure the deed has been transferred properly.

18. Redirect your mail to your new address.

19. Decorate with paint, shelving, etc.

20. Take pictures or record a video of your new home and belongings to give to the insurance company.

21. Most of all, *relax*! You deserve it.

Additionally, there are items that you should always keep around your home just in case of an emergency. I call it the "smart home shoppers list." The next time you go to the store, be sure to throw these items in your cart.

- Candles

- Matches or lighters

- Blankets

- Light bulbs

- Flashlight

- Rope

- A hunting knife

- Ladder

- Batteries

- An assortment of screwdrivers

- At least one case of water

- Canned foods

• Manual can opener

These are items that you should have in your home at all times just in case you need them. And if there is ever a local or regional state of emergency, such as a blackout or flood, you will have the bare necessities to tide you over.

I hope I've simplified the home-buying process for you to feel confident about taking the leap. There's no doubt that buying a house is one of the biggest purchases of your life, but remember to keep calm . . . you *can* do this. Not just anyone can buy a house, especially these days. It takes a very, very special and prepared person to be able to close the deal, which is a good thing, at least in *my* book! The handy index at the end should help you skip straight to the sections you need for reference.

And speaking of my book, I really want this to be *your* book. I hope this becomes your go-to guide for every step that must be taken on your road to homeownership. I don't expect you to memorize my tips and explanations. But keep the book handy. When the time comes for a brushup, just go back and reread the chapter pertaining to the milestone you have reached. The saying, *"Cross that bridge when you get to it"* applies here, meaning you can always open up to the chapter you need right before you are ready to take that step.

Here's my last bit of advice: Never get so discouraged that you give up! If owning your own home is your dream, you can make it happen. For some people, the whole process of buying a home is scary and foreign; whereas, others will enjoy it enough to do it again and again throughout their lives. I hope you are one of those people who find *joy* and *happiness* when it comes to buying your own piece of the earth.

My last hope for you is that you will share your joy of homeownership with me, either by emailing me at **Egypt@ EgyptSherrodRealEstate.com,** visiting my website, **www.Egypt SherrodRealEstate.com**, or leaving a comment on my Facebook page, **facebook.com/EgyptSherrod**. If you enjoy the book as much as I hope you do, take a photo of yourself holding the book and tag me on **Instagram @EgyptSherrod**. Even if I don't know you personally, I feel a strong bond with you already. After all, I wrote this book entirely for *you*!

THE LINGO:
Real Estate Terms to Know

Adjustable-Rate Mortgage (ARM)

A mortgage that changes interest rates periodically, in accordance with fluctuations in the index in which the ARM is associated with.

Adjustment Date

A specified date of adjustment to the interest rate on an adjustable-rate (ARM) mortgage.

Amortization

A loan repayment includes a portion of the loan that will be applied to pay the interest accrued on the loan, with the remainder to be applied on the loan's principal. Over time, the interest payment decreases in conjunction with the loan balance. The principal amount also increases (amortizes) to pay off the loan within the designated period of time.

Amortization Schedule

A chart that indicates how much of a percentage or amount of each payment will be applied toward the principal and the interest over the duration of the loan. This table also reveals the gradual decrease of the loan balance until it reaches zero.

Annual Percentage Rate (APR)

APR is a value that adheres to a government formula designed to reflect the actual yearly cost of borrowing. It is expressed as a percentage and typically can be figured by deducting the closing costs of the loan, then taking the loan payment and factoring the interest rate to figure out the annual percentage rate. The APR is higher than your your mortgage rate because you will make the same payment on a smaller amount. This does not reflect the true rate of your loan and is merely a guideline.

Application

To apply for a mortgage loan, the individual fills in this form, which collects information about the borrower. This may include bank accounts, assets, debts, employment history, and other financial details.

Appraisal

A professionally prepared justification of the value or price of a property, based mainly on an analysis of similar home sales within the vicinity of the property.

Appraised Value

An evaluation of a property's fair market value, based on the analysis, knowledge, and experience of the property appraiser. An appraisal is based largely on comparable sales. It is a "professional opinion" that the purchase price falls in line with current market value.

Appraiser

A person with the knowledge, education, training, and expertise to evaluate the value of any given property. Appraisers can be individuals working independently or directly for mortgage lenders.

Appreciation

The increase in property value due to fluctuations in the economy, market inflation, or other reasons.

Assessed Value

The amount of a property's value deemed by a public tax assessor for purposes of annual property taxes.

Assessment

The actual value that is placed on a property for the purposes of taxation.

Assessor

A public official who uses criteria to estimate the value of a property for tax purposes.

Assets

The items of value that an individual owns. These can be converted to cash as "liquid assets" and may include stocks or bonds, savings accounts, mutual funds, real estate, personal property, and other items that can be sold if funds are needed.

Balloon Mortgage

A mortgage loan that requires the balance of the principal to be paid by certain date; for instance, a loan that is amortized over twenty-five years, but by the fifteenth year demands the remainder of the balance be paid. The term "balloon" implies "inflating" payment.

Balloon Payment

The final lump sum payment due by the specified date of a balloon mortgage.

Bill of Sale

In real estate lingo, this is the written document that transfers the title of personal property from one owner to another.

Biweekly Mortgage

A setup by the mortgage lender that allows you to make payments every other week, instead of just once a month. By doing this, you will actually make thirteen payments during the year instead of twelve, which can greatly reduce the principal over time.

Breach of Contract

When the terms and conditions of a legal contract are not adhered to, this is known as a breach of contract.

Broker

In a real estate context, a real estate broker is also known as an "agent" or "broker," which can be one in the same. More specifically, a broker is someone who serves as an agent to bring two parties together for the sake of a transaction, resulting in a commission or fee for their role.

Buydown

This is a mortgage financing technique in which the buyer can obtain a lower interest rate during the first few years of the loan by having the seller make payments to the mortgage lending institution. This subsequently reduces the buyer's monthly interest rate and payment.

Buyer's Agent

A real estate agent who represents the homebuyer in a real estate transaction; their primary responsibility is in upholding the buyer's best interests.

Certificate of Eligibility

A document issued by the Veterans Administration that certifies a veteran's eligibility for a VA loan.

Certificate of Reasonable Value (CRV)

After an appraisal has been completed on a property being purchased through a VA loan, the Veterans Administration then issues a CRV.

Chain of Title

A document that lists all of the known transfers of title holders on a piece of property since it was first built or purchased.

Clear Title

A title that does not have any property liens or companies claiming to hold ownership of the property or any part of it.

Closing

Depending on which state you live in, the "closing" is the date in which a real estate transaction is finalized and the documents recorded at a local municipality. A "closing" can also be known as the designated day in which all of the documents in a home sale are prepared and signed, and when the money for the purchase changes hands.

Closing Costs

Closing costs are separated into two categories. "Nonrecurring closing costs" are any items paid one time as a result of buying the property or per the terms of the loan. "Pre-paids" are any items that recur over time, such as property taxes, HOA dues, or homeowners insurance.

The lender will make an estimate of the non-recurring closing costs and prepaid items on what is known as a "good faith estimate" that is issued to the borrower within three days of their receipt of the loan application.

Cloud on Title

If any conditions are found during a title search that could potentially affect the smooth transition of the real estate title to the purchaser, this is called a cloud. Clouds on a title can only be removed by court action, issuing a new deed, or release of the cloud on the property title.

Co-borrower

A second individual listed on the title to the property, who is also responsible for the mortgage payments. It is common in marriages for both spouses to share ownership.

Collateral

In a home loan, the property itself is the collateral. Therefore, if the loan is not repaid in accordance with the mortgage terms, the borrower risks losing the mortgage or deed of trust.

Collection

A loan goes into "collection" if a borrower falls behind on their mortgage payments. The lender is asked to mail and record certain documents, just in case the bank forecloses on the property.

Commission

Sales people, brokers, agents, and other industry professionals earn a commission for their involvement in the real estate transaction. The commission is paid by the seller or buyer, depending on the terms of the sale.

Common Areas

Sections of a land, buildings, and amenities that are owned or managed by a homeowners association. Common areas are used by all of the unit owners, who share in the overall operational and maintenance expenses. These may include clubhouses, swimming pools, basketball courts, parking areas, and other recreational space, or the use of facilities.

Comparable Sales

An "apples to apples" comparison of recently sold properties in neighboring areas, which is used to determine the fair market value of the property. Also known as "comps."

Comparative Market Analysis (CMA)

A document that averages out the selling price of recently sold homes in the area (the "fair market" value), the CMA is a powerful negotiating tool during the bidding process.

Condominium

A type of ownership in which the common areas of a property are jointly shared, except for the interior of the private, individual unit to which the buyer holds the title. Also called a "condo," this term actually refers to the type of ownership, rather than the building itself.

Construction Loan

A short-term loan obtained by a builder in order to finance the cost of construction. The lender makes payments to the builder at periodic intervals as the work progresses.

Contingency

A condition that must be met before a contract becomes legally binding. For example, home purchasers may request a contingency that states the contract is not legally binding until the buyer gets a satisfactory home inspection report from a qualified home inspector.

Contract

A written agreement that is agreed to and signed by two or more parties.

Conventional Mortgage

Any home loan that does not fall under the category of government loans (VA and FHA).

Convertible ARM

An adjustable-rate mortgage that enables the borrower to change the ARM to a fixed-rate mortgage if done within a specific period of time.

Cooperative (Co-op)

A type of multiple ownership in which residents of a multi-unit housing complex each own a share of it in cooperation with the main share-holder. Each individual resident has occupancy of a designated apart-ment or unit.

Covenants, Conditions, and Restrictions

Mutual covenants between members of a homeowners association (HOA) are pledges to abide by the rules of conduct or restrictions on the use of their property. The rules are designed to govern peaceful use, with association restrictions imposed on new construction or use of the property, parking, etc. These covenants, conditions, and restrictions are most common within a gated community, a development, or a condominium complex.

Credit

An agreement in which a borrower receives something of value in exchange for a promise to repay the lender at a later date.

Credit History

A record of a person's debt repayment history, including both timely and late repayment of debt. The histories are managed by three major credit bureaus and can be pulled for review to enable a lender to determine the individual's risk of default.

Creditor

A person to whom money is owed.

Credit Report

A professional report about a person's individual credit history, which is prepared by a credit bureau and used by a lender in deciding upon a borrower's credit worthiness.

Deed

The legal document conveying title ownership to a property.

Deed-in-Lieu

Short for "deed in lieu of foreclosure," this transfers the title to the lender if the borrower defaults on the loan and wants to avoid foreclosure. If the borrower asks for a deed-in-lieu, the lender may choose to cease the foreclosure process. Regardless of whether the lender accepts the offer, the non-repayment or avoidance of debt will most likely remain on the person's credit history. However, a deed-in-lieu may stall or halt the preparation of documents before a foreclosure enters the public record.

Deed of Trust
Some states record a deed of trust instead of a mortgage, but the term carries the same meaning.

Default
If payment on a first mortgage has not been made within thirty days (or specified time frame in the contract) of the due date, the loan goes into default.

Deposit
The sum of money put down in advance of a larger amount as a good faith act that the rest will follow upon the signing of the contract.

Depreciation
When the value of a property declines, it is known as depreciation.

Discount Points
Regarding mortgages, this term is used in reference to government loans, such as FHA and VA loans. Discount points refer to the "points" paid in addition to one percent of the loan origination fee. A "point" is one percent of the loan amount.

Down Payment
The "up-front" money that a buyer applies to the purchase of a property. The down payment is not considered part of the purchase amount financed by the lender.

Dual Disclosed Agency

A real estate agent/broker who serves as both an agent for the buyer and seller with an agreement and obligation to satisfy both. In some states, disclosed dual-agency is not allowed, but in other states it must be known and agreed to in writing by both parties.

Earnest Money Deposit

A deposit made by a potential homebuyer to show they are serious about the purchase of the home.

Equity

A homeowner's financial interest in a property, derived by taking the fair market value of the home and subtracting that amount from what is still owed to the lender. If a home has increased in value, it has equity.

Escrow

When something of value, such as money or documents, is deposited by an impartial person or organization, this is known as an escrow. The escrow is to be given to the intended party upon fulfillment of a condition. In real estate, the earnest money deposit is placed into escrow and then delivered to the seller on the closing day.

Escrow Account

Even after the purchase of a property, you may have an escrow account set up with the lender, which covers things like property taxes and insurance. You pay extra each month above what is required of the loan obligation, but the extra funds are held in an escrow account and only released when the time comes for these items to be paid. The lender then makes the payments on your behalf to save you stress of saving up to pay these annual bills.

Eviction
The lawful expulsion of an occupant from real estate property.

Examination of Title
A report made on the title of a property, taken from either an abstract of the title or from public records.

Exclusive Listing
A written contract that allows a licensed real estate agent to market, show, and sell a property exclusively for a buyer over a specified time period.

Fair Market Value
The average selling price of recently sold homes in the area. It is often the highest price that a buyer is willing to pay and the lowest a seller is willing to accept.

Fannie Mae (FNMA)
The Federal National Mortgage Association (FNMA) is a congressionally chartered, shareholder-owned company and is the largest lender of mortgages in the nation.

Fannie Mae's Community Homebuyer's Program
This community lending model is based on the income of the borrower under which mortgage insurers and Fannie Mae offer looser

underwriting guidelines to enable low-to-moderate-income families to buy a home. It works by decreasing the total amount of cash needed to purchase a home. Buyers who take part in this program are required to attend mandatory pre-purchase homebuyer education workshops.

Federal Housing Administration (FHA)

A US Department of Housing and Urban Development (HUD) agency, the FHA's primary job is to insure residential mortgage loans made by private lenders. The FHA has standards in place for construction and underwriting, but does not lend money or do the actual construction of housing.

FHA Mortgage

A mortgage insured by the Federal Housing Administration (FHA). In addition to VA loans, an FHA loan is referred to as a government loan.

Firm Commitment

A lender's agreement to make a loan to a certain borrower for a specific property.

First Mortgage

The mortgage in the first line among any loans recorded against the property. This often refers to the date in which a loan is recorded.

Fixed-rate Mortgage

A mortgage that locks in the interest rate with firm resolve for the entire term of the loan.

Flood Insurance

Insurance that reimburses the homeowner for any physical property damage occurring directly from flooding. It is mandatory for properties that are located in federally designated flood zones.

Foreclosure

A legal process by which a borrower is in default of their mortgage agreement and is therefore forced to sell it at a public auction (whether they want to or not). The proceeds of the auction are then applied to the mortgage debt and the bidder becomes the current owner.

Hazard Insurance

In the event of physical damage to a property, hazard insurance covers destruction from fire, extreme weather, wind, and other hazards.

Home Equity Conversion Mortgage (HECM)

Also called "reverse annuity mortgage," a HECM is unique in that instead of making payments to a lender, the lender makes payments to you. Particularly for homeowners who have acquired equity, they can con-vert the equity into cash in the form of monthly payments. Unlike typical home equity loans, the borrower does not qualify on the basis of income alone, rather on the value of the property. This type of loan does not have to be repaid until the borrower no longer occupies the property.

Home Equity Line of Credit (HELOC)

A second mortgage loan that allows the borrower to acquire cash drawn against the property's equity, up to a specified amount.

Home Inspection

A comprehensive inspection performed by a professional evaluator of both the structural and mechanical conditions of a property. A satisfactory home inspection is sometimes included as a contingency by the purchaser to ensure the home meets expected standards.

Homeowners Association (HOA)

A corporation that is made by a real estate developer for the purposes of management, marketing, and selling homes and lots in a residential subdivision. It gives the developer privileged voting rights in governing the HOA, while allowing them to avoid other financial and legal responsibility for the organization. The HOA transfers ownership to the homeowners after selling off a certain number of lots. Membership in a homeowners association is a condition of the purchase; therefore, the buyer is not given an option to object to the membership. In return, they are privileged to special opportunities within the HOA's territory.

Homeowners Insurance

An insurance policy combining personal liability insurance with hazard insurance coverage for a building and its contents.

Homeowners Warranty

A type of insurance bought by homebuyers to cover repairs to bigger items, in case they break. The buyer can ask the seller for this type of coverage as part of the sale, but either party can pay.

HUD Home

When a home with a government-insured FHA mortgage is foreclosed, ownership is transferred to the US Department of Housing and Home Development and becomes a "HUD" property. Many foreclosures are HUD homes.

Lease

A written agreement between a property owner and a renter that outlines the payment and conditions under which the renter may live in or use the property for a specified period of time, which can then be extended if the owner chooses.

Lease Option

An alternative financing solution that enables homebuyers to lease a home with an option to buy it later. Each month's rent payment can include the rent plus an additional amount that is applied toward the down payment of a predetermined and agreed-upon purchase price.

Lender

The organization, individual, or institution who loans money. A loan officer is also commonly known as a lender.

Liabilities

An individual's financial obligations. Liabilities include both long- and short-term debt, as well as amounts owed to others, such as an auto loan or credit card debt.

Liability Insurance

Insurance coverage that gives protection against claims due to a property owner's negligence or inappropriate actions that may result in bodily injury or property damage to another individual. This is often part of the homeowners insurance policy.

Lien

A legal claim against a property that must be paid before the property can be sold. The first mortgage deed is considered a lien, but liens can also be placed upon a property if, for example, the owner fails to pay property taxes or defaults on other financial obligations tied to the home.

Lien Holder

A lien holder is an individual or entity who has a lien (or claim) on a particular property. A claim is made by a binding agreement, such as a mortgage loan. The lien amount can either equal or exceed the market value of the property since the extra portion of the lien's value is considered an unsecured debt.

Loan

An amount of money that is borrowed from an individual or institution and is typically repaid with interest accrued as a benefit to the lender.

Loan Officer

An account representative (also known as a "lender") who prepares the paperwork and makes the decisions on each applicant's worthiness of a loan. The loan officer has varied responsibilities, including selling the loan, representing the lending institution, and representing the borrower with assistance to obtain the loan.

Loan Origination

The process of obtaining new loans.

Loan Servicing

After getting a loan, the companies you make payments to are the ones "servicing" your loan. They process payments, manage the escrow and distribution of funds, send up-to-date statements, make collection efforts on overdue accounts, and provide a plethora of other services.

Loan-to-value (LTV)

The percentage relationship between the amount of a loan and its sales price or appraised value (whichever is less).

Lock-in

A binding agreement in which a lender guarantees a set interest rate for a specified period of time at a predetermined cost.

Lock-in Period

A period of time in which the lender has guaranteed a locked-in interest rate to the borrower.

Mortgage

A legal document that offers a specified property to a mortgage lender as collateral of a debt. Also known as a "Deed of Trust" in some states.

Mortgage Banker

A mortgage banker is an individual or entity that originates and funds its own loans. The mortgage loans are then sold on the secondary market to Fannie Mae, Freddie Mac, or Ginnie Mae, and other mortgage programs. This term can apply loosely to both mortgage bankers and mortgage brokers or firms.

Mortgage Broker

A mortgage company that originates mortgage loans and then offers them to lending institutions with which they have pre-established relationships.

Mortgagee

In a mortgage agreement, this refers to the lender.

Mortgage Insurance (MI)

Insurance covering the lender against losses incurred as a result of a default on a home loan. Mortgage insurance is typically mandatory on all home loans that have a loan-to-value higher than 80 percent. FHA loans and other first-time homebuyer programs often require mortgage insurance, regardless of the loan-to-value.

Mortgage Insurance Premium (MIP)

The amount paid by a borrower for mortgage insurance, either to a government agency (such as the Federal Housing Administration) or to a private mortgage insurance company.

No-Cost Loan

Some lenders offer mortgages at "no cost," meaning the costs that you would typically associate with a purchase or refinance transaction are waived. These fees could include title insurance, recording documents, fees, escrow fees, settlements, appraisals, notary dues, and others. Be aware that the interest rate may be higher than if you get a loan with costs built in.

Note

A legal document that defines the borrower's obligation to repay a mortgage loan at a specific rate for a designated period of time.

Note Rate

The interest rate stated on a mortgage note.

No-Points Loan

Nearly all lenders offer loans with "no points," meaning the interest rate is about a quarter percent higher than on a loan where one point is paid up front.

Original Principal Balance

The total amount of principal owed on a mortgage before any payments are made.

Origination Fee

For government loans, the loan origination fee is one percent of the loan amount. On a conventional loan, the loan origination fee describes the total number of points a borrower pays.

Owner Financing

In some cases, a seller may provide all or a portion of the financing to the right buyer, which is called owner financing. Instead of making payments to a lending institution, the tenant makes payments to the owner of the property with the intent to buy.

PITI

This is an acronym for principal, interest, taxes and insurance. Your monthly payment to the lender includes all of these things, plus mortgage insurance in many cases. The lender uses this formula to determine your debt-to-income ratio.

PITI Reserves

The cash amount that a borrower is required to have in savings after making a down payment and paying all closing costs to buy a home. The PITI reserves must equal the amount that the borrower would have to pay for PITI for a predesignated number of months.

Planned Unit Development (PUD)

A type of ownership in which people unite to own a building or compound they live in, but where common areas are jointly owned by members of the development or association. Unlike condominiums, where a person only owns the immediate space of his unit, the buildings and common areas of a PUD are shared with all of the individual owners.

Preapproved

A loose term to describe a borrower who has completed a loan application prior to shopping for a home. It means their application has been reviewed and approved up to a designated amount specified by the lender/underwriter.

Prepayment

An amount paid to lessen the principal balance of a loan before the due date. This may result from a sale of the property or by the homeowner's decision to pay off the loan in full. Prepayment means that full payment was made before the loan's deadline.

Prepayment Penalty

Some loans are written with a clause that if a borrower pays the loan off early, then they will be required to pay a "fee" or a penalty for doing so.

Prequalification

A loan officer's written opinion of the borrower's ability to qualify for a home loan, based on information about debt, income, and savings. This is a more informal assessment than preapproval.

Prime Rate

A special interest rate that banks offer only to premium customers. Changes in the prime rate are used as the index in many adjustable rate mortgages, especially home equity loans.

Principal

The original amount borrowed, or the portion of the monthly mortgage payment that reduces the remaining balance of a mortgage.

Principal Balance

The outstanding balance of principal on a mortgage. The principal balance does not reflect any interest or other charges.

Private Mortgage Insurance (PMI)

Mortgage insurance that is offered by a private mortgage insurance company to protect lenders against loss if the buyer defaults. Most lenders require PMI for a mortgage loan until 20 percent of the principal has been paid down.

Property Taxes

A government levy on property that each property owner is required to pay. Property taxes are levied by the governing authorities within each jurisdiction. These may include national government, federated state, county/geographical regions, or municipalities. Multiple jurisdictions can also tax the same property, depending on its location.

Public Auction

A publicly announced meeting at a courthouse or public location with the intent to sell a property for the purpose of repaying a mortgage loan that is in default (i.e., a foreclosed home). The individual who buys the property at an auction then becomes responsible for it, including any claims or liens.

Purchase Agreement

A written contract signed by both the buyer and seller that states the terms and conditions under which a property will be sold.

Rate Lock

A commitment made by a lender to a borrower that guarantees the interest rate to be locked in for a specified period of time.

Real Estate Agent

A person licensed to show, market, negotiate, and transact the purchase or sale of real estate.

Real Estate Settlement Procedures Act (RESPA)

A consumer protection law that requires lenders to give borrowers advance notice of how much closing costs will be.

Real Property

Land and appurtenances, including anything of a permanent nature such as structures, trees, minerals, and the interest, benefits, and inherent rights thereof.

Realtor

A real estate broker, agent, or associate who has an active membership on a local real estate board or affiliation with the National Association of Realtors.

Second Mortgage

A mortgage that is underneath a first mortgage with a lien position.

Seller's Agent

An agent who represents the seller in a real estate transaction. Their fiduciary responsibility is to the seller.

Short Sale

The sale of a real estate property in which the proceeds fall short of the actual balance of debt on the property, usually because the property owner cannot afford to repay the debt per the terms of the contract. Therefore, the lender agrees to release the obligations on the real estate by accepting less than what is owed. This is often a better solution than foreclosure, since the lender gets back part of its investment and the borrower has a less negative mark against his or her credit history.

Subdivision

A housing development designed by subplotting a parcel of land into individual lots for sale or lease, most commonly to build new homes.

Survey

A drawing or map that shows the precise legal boundaries of a property. It reveals the right of way, easements, encroachments, and any other physical characteristics.

Tax Lien

A lien imposed lawfully upon a property to secure the payment of property taxes. A tax lien may be imposed when the property owner becomes delinquent in paying taxes owed on real or personal property. It may also result from a failure to pay income taxes.

Title

A legal document that shows an individual's ownership of a specific property.

Title Company

A company specializing in examination of titles of a real estate property, including any liens, claims, or other potential hassles.

Title Insurance

Insurance protecting the lender or buyer against any losses arising from disputes over ownership of a property.

Title Search

A check of the history of the title of a property against the records to make sure that the seller is the legal owner of the property and that no liens or claims to it remain outstanding by previous owners.

Transfer of Ownership

Any means by which ownership of a property changes from one person or entity to another.

Transfer Tax

A state or local tax that is payable to the government or municipality once the title passes from one owner to another.

Under Contract

When a house is under contract, an agreement exists between a buyer and seller that states the seller may not enter into a contractual agreement with any other buyer, usually after the purchaser has allocated funds for a down payment, which are held in escrow while the contract is being finalized. The buyer is also obligated to purchase the property from the seller when it is under contract.

Underwriter

An insurance company that issues insurance policies to the general public or to another insurer.

Veterans Administration Mortgage

A mortgage that is guaranteed by the Department of Veterans Affairs (VA), available to eligible veterans and their spouses.

Veterans Administration (VA)

A federal agency of the US government that guarantees residential mortgages made to eligible veterans of the military. This guarantee protects the lender against loss and therefore encourages them to give mortgage loans to veterans.

ACKNOWLEDGMENTS

"Alone we can do so little,
Together we can do so much."
—HELEN KELLER

THIS BOOK WOULD NOT BE POSSIBLE WITHOUT the guidance and contributions of some pretty ROCK-STAR people.

To my business partner and soul sister, Amber Noble Garland, thank you for your tireless commitment, raw honesty, tough love, and sisterhood. We are great on our own, but we are unstoppable together!

Jennifer Kasius, my editor, thank you for believing in my voice and vision from the very start! I could not have asked for a better coach through this experience.

Many thanks to Allen Cooley for the fantastic cover

photo, Frances Soo Ping Chow for the vibrant cover design, Amanda Richmond for designing the interior, Amy Cianfrone for being such a dream to work with, and to the entire Running Press Team.

It truly takes a village! And to my village at CAA, Cait Hoyt and Adam Nettler—Thank you! To Kristen Cooper, Bridgit Crider, and Stephanie Jacobs. You ladies help me to shine! Teamwork makes the dreamwork.

Immense gratitude goes out to Heather Weiss and Alex O'Neill at Much & House PR as well as Rebecca Brooks and the team and Brooks Group PR.

Thanks Anne Violette, you truly are a gem. And to my fellow Realtors,® keep shining!

To my Egypt Sherrod Real Estate Group clients who've given me the privilege of guiding them on their journey to homeownership, and to the loyal *Property Virgins* viewers.

Lastly, thank you to the incredible team at Cineflix and HGTV. From, the production assistants, producers, directors, editors, all the way up to my executives—Thank you for the countless hours spent making *Property Virgins* such a hit, therefore making this book possible.

INDEX

A

Adjustable-rate mortgage (ARM), 103–105, 185
Adjustment date, 104, 185
Affordable Housing Partnership Program (AHPP), 81–82
Amortization, 185–186
Amortization schedule, 186
Annual percentage rate (APR), 186
Anonymous sellers, 76
Appraisals, 140–146
    appraised value, 144–145, 187
    benefits of, 140–141
    components of, 143–144
    contingencies on, 146
    cost approach to, 142
    cost of, 141
    definition of, 186
    low appraisals, 144–146
    methods of, 141–142
    sales-comparison approach to, 142
Appraised value, 144–145, 187
Appraiser, 141–146, 187
Appreciation rates, 26, 187
Assessed value, 187
Assessment, 131, 142, 187
Assessor, 187
Assets, 89, 187–188
Attorney fees, 20, 116, 121
Attorney, hiring, 116–122, 157

B

Balloon mortgage, 188
Balloon payment, 188
Bidding strategies, 111–116
Bidding wars, 112–116
Bill of sale, 188

Bills, paying on time, 93, 95
Biweekly mortgage, 188
Breach of contract, 188. *See also* Contract
Brokers, 37–40, 189
Budget. *See also* Financial matters
    creating, 19, 177
    financial comfort zone, 20, 83, 116, 151–152, 176
    living expenses, 151–154
    sticking with, 20, 52–54, 59, 63, 87
Building contractors, 75
Buydown, 189
Buyer's agents, 11, 35–36, 189.
    See also Real estate agents
Buyers' market, 74
Bylaws, 60–63

C

Car loans, 95, 173
Career stability, 19, 92–93
Certificate of eligibility, 189
Certificate of reasonable value (CRV), 189
Chain of title, 163, 189
Clear deed, 72, 167
Clear title, 72, 167, 190. *See also* Title company
Closing costs, 20, 93, 107, 120, 170, 190
Closing process, 169–177
    attorney for, 157
    costs for, 20, 93, 107, 120, 170, 190
    definition of, 190
    delays in, 171
    documents for, 170–171
    finalizing, 178
    homeowners insurance for, 169–170, 173–176

private mortgage insurance
for, 177
reviewing, 170–171
Co-borrower, 191
Collateral, 115, 191
Collection, 191
Comfort zone, 20, 23, 83, 15
1–152, 176
Commission, 36–37, 45, 191
Community
bonding with, 27
common areas in, 58, 62, 191
gated community, 58–64
HOA community, 58–64
schools in, 49, 54, 56–57
touring, 56–57
Comparable sales, 125–126,
142–143, 192
Comparative market analysis
(CMA), 125–126, 142–143, 192
Condominium, 192
Construction companies, 75
Construction loan, 192
Contingencies, 115, 138–139,
146, 192
Contingency plans, 18–19, 84
Contract
assistance with, 117, 120–121
breach of, 188
definition of, 193
mortgage commitment, 90–91
purchase agreement, 137, 145, 208
reviewing, 170–171
"under contract," 90, 211
Conventional loans, 101–103, 193
Convertible ARM, 193
Cooperative (co-op), 193
Costs. See also Down payment
attorney fees, 20, 116, 121
closing costs, 20, 93, 107, 120, 170, 190
HOA fees, 59, 62–63
home appraisal cost, 141

home inspection cost, 124, 129, 136
homeowners insurance cost, 168
of homeownership, 20, 24
loan origination fee, 205
mortgage application fee, 89
moving costs, 20
title fees, 20, 167–168
Covenants, 62, 119, 193
Credit, 194
Credit card companies, 95, 97
Credit card debt, 92, 95–99
Credit card limits, 92, 95
Credit history, 93, 194
Credit reports, 92–94, 97–99, 194
Credit score
damaging, 98–99
FICO score, 94
improving, 25, 94–97
maintaining, 92, 94–97
mortgage payments and, 25
Creditors, 94, 97, 194
Curb appeal, 10, 143

D

Debt-to-credit ratio, 95–96, 98
Debt-to-income ratio, 115
Deed, clear, 72, 167, 194
Deed-in-lieu, 194
Deed of trust, 195
Deed, recording, 157
Default, 69–71, 74, 81–83, 96, 105–108,
195
Deposit, 137, 159–160, 195, 196
Depreciation, 142, 195
Discount points, 195
Distressed properties, 65–79
explanation of, 65–67
foreclosures, 65–72, 199
public auctions, 66–69, 208
REO properties, 66
short sales, 65–72, 210

upside-down properties, 71, 77
Down payment, 80–87
  advantages of, 83
  amount required for, 82–85, 101–103
  definition of, 195
  as equity in home, 83
  for first-time homebuyers, 81–82
  importance of, 80–81
  saving, 18, 84–85, 93, 153–154
Dual disclosed agents, 35–36, 44, 196.
  See also Real estate agents
Due diligence period, 135

E

Earnest money deposit, 137,
  159–160, 195, 196
Easements, 159
Emergency fund, 152–154
Enthusiasm, curbing, 148, 150
Equity, 26, 83, 196. *See also* Home
  equity loan
Escrow, 159–160, 196
Escrow account, 196–197
Eviction, 70, 117, 197
Exclusive listings, 197
Expired listings, 78

F

Fair market value, 197
Fannie Mae, 102, 197–198
Federal Home Loan Mortgage
  Corporation (FHLMC), 102
Federal Housing Administration
  (FHA), 82, 101, 198
Federal National Mortgage
  Association (FNMA), 102, 197
Fees. *See also* Costs
  attorney fees, 20, 116, 121
  HOA fees, 59, 62–63
  home appraisal fee, 141
  home inspection fee, 124, 129, 136

loan origination fee, 205
mortgage application fee, 89
title fees, 20, 167–168
FHA loan, 82, 100–103, 105–106, 198
FICO score, 94. *See also* Credit score
Financial matters
  budget, 19–20, 52–54, 59, 63, 87
  comfort zone, 20, 83, 116, 151–152, 176
  contingency plans, 18–19, 84
  down payment, 18, 80–87, 93, 101–103,
  153–154
  emergency fund, 152–154
  mortgage preapproval, 88–109
  savings account, 74, 83–84, 93, 115,
  152–154
  "walkaway number," 116
Firm commitment, 90–91, 198
First mortgage, 108, 198
First-time homebuyers, 18, 81–82,
  101–106, 154–155
Fixed-rate mortgage, 27, 103–105, 198
Flexibility, 15, 115–116
Flipping properties, 10, 125
Flood insurance, 175, 199
"For sale by owner" (FSBO), 79
Foreclosures, 65–72, 199
Freddie Mac, 102
Furnishings, purchasing, 154
Furnishings, saving for, 153–154

G

Gated communities, 58–64
Gem properties, 111, 125
Glossary of terms, 185–212
Goals, setting, 17–18
Good faith estimate, 120, 170
Graduated payment loan, 106

H

Hazard insurance, 175, 199
HOA amenities, 59
HOA community, 58–64
HOA fees, 59, 62–63
HOA rules, 59–63
Home
  bidding strategies on, 111–116
  clear title to, 72, 166–167
  closing process for, 169–177
  condition of, 55
  easements for, 159
  history of, 55, 139
  inspection of, 123–139
  insurance on, 24, 27, 128, 168–170,
    173–176, 200
  liens on, 66, 70, 72, 159, 162
  location of, 11, 49, 56–58, 150
  maintenance tasks for, 19, 24, 180–182
  making offer on, 110–122, 148–149
  new home, 18–20, 75
  previously owned homes, 18–20
  resale value of, 56, 125, 150–151
  restrictions on, 159, 193
  supplies for, 182–183
  "under contract," 90, 211
  walk-through inspection of, 170
  years living in, 18
Home appraisal, 140–146
  appraised value, 144–145, 187
  appraisers, 141–146, 187
  benefits of, 140–141
  components of, 143–144
  contingencies on, 146
  cost approach to, 142
  cost of, 141
  low appraisals, 144–146
  methods of, 141–142
  sales-comparison approach to, 142
Home-buying process, 14–28
  advice on, 16–21
  avoiding pitfalls, 147–156
  bidding strategies, 111–116
  closing process, 169–177
  contingencies, 115, 138–139
  factors to consider, 17–21
  first-time homebuyers, 18, 81–82,
    101–106, 154–155
  flexibility in, 15, 115–116
  home appraisal, 140–146
  home inspection, 123–139
  joint home purchase, 155–156
  making offers, 110–122, 148–149
  planning for, 20–21
  pros/cons of, 20–21
  reasons for purchase, 18, 24
  ruining, 149
  title companies, 157–168
  understanding, 8–9
  "walkaway number," 116
Home construction, 75
Home construction loan, 192
Home equity conversion mortgage
  (HECM), 199
Home equity line of credit
  (HELOC), 199
Home equity loan, 107–109, 199
Home-finding process, 47–64
  anonymous sellers, 76
  distressed properties, 65–79
  expired listings, 78
  "for sale by owner" homes, 79
  foreclosures, 65–72, 199
  gated communities, 58–64
  inventory shortages, 73–79
  location of home, 49, 56–58
  "Make Me Move" listings, 76
  narrowing home choices, 49–52
  networking, 78
  organizing search, 48–49
  photos of, 49
  pocket listings, 76
  pre-market listings, 77

rental properties, 77
short sales, 65–72, 210
supply and demand, 72–75, 112
upside-down properties, 71, 77
viewing homes, 50–52
withdrawn listings, 77–78
Home inspections, 123–139
  areas inspected, 133–135
  being present during, 136–137
  contingencies on, 138–139
  cost of, 124, 129, 136
  definition of, 200
  earnest money deposit and, 137
  failure of, 137
  final inspection, 170
  hiring inspector, 123–124, 127–133, 136
  importance of, 123–139
  report from, 136–137
  skipping, 126–129, 138
  time required for, 136
  timeframe for, 135
Home inspector
  certified inspectors, 126, 130–135
  finding, 132–133
  hiring, 123–124, 127–133, 136
Home maintenance tasks, 19, 24, 180–182
Homeowners Association (HOA),
  58–64, 200
Homeowners insurance, 24, 27, 128,
  168–170, 173–176, 200
Homeowners warranty, 200
Homeownership
  attaining, 178–184
  benefits of, 25–28
  costs of, 20, 24
  finalizing closing, 178
  keys to home, 179–180
  pride of, 27
  reasons for, 18, 24–28
  supplies for home, 182–183
  tasks to perform, 180–182
  tips on, 179–184

transfer of, 211
Homeownership Assistance Program
  (HOAP), 81
House-hunting process, 47–64
  anonymous sellers, 76
  distressed properties, 65–79
  expired listings, 78
  "for sale by owner" homes, 79
  foreclosures, 65–72, 199
  gated communities, 58–64
  inventory shortages, 73–79
  location of home, 49, 56–58
  "Make Me Move" listings, 76
  narrowing home choices, 49–52
  networking, 78
  organizing search, 48–49
  photos of, 49
  pocket listings, 76
  pre-market listings, 77
  rental properties, 77
  short sales, 65–72, 210
  supply and demand, 72–75, 112
  upside-down properties, 71, 77
  viewing homes, 50–52
  withdrawn listings, 77–78
"House poor," 83, 152
Housing appreciation, 26, 187
Housing bubble, 71, 74–75
Housing demand, 26, 72–75, 112
Housing market
  crisis in, 31, 71, 74–75, 81, 101, 130
  cycles in, 72–75
  fluctuations in, 16, 26
  housing demand, 26, 72–75, 112
  inventory shortages, 73–79
  supply and demand, 72–75, 112
Housing shortages, 73–79
HUD home, 81, 200–201

I

Income-to-debt ratio, 92, 115
Insurance
    cost of, 24, 27
    flood insurance, 175, 199
    hazard insurance, 175, 199
    homeowners insurance, 24, 27, 128, 168–170, 173–176, 200
    liability insurance, 201–202
    mortgage insurance, 204
    private mortgage insurance, 83, 85, 102–103, 107, 177, 208
    title insurance, 161–168
Interest rates
    adjustable rates, 103–105, 185
    annual percentage rate, 186
    fixed rates, 27, 103–105, 198
    locking in, 89, 105, 203, 209
    low rates, 105, 107
    prime rate, 207
Inventory shortages, 73–79

J

Job stability, 19, 92–93
Joint home purchase, 155–156

L

Lease option, 201
Leases, 77, 159, 201
Lender, 42, 82–84, 100–107, 201
Liabilities, 201
Liability insurance, 201–202
Liens
    foreclosures and, 70
    short sales and, 66
    tax liens, 37, 72, 164, 202, 210
    title search on, 159, 162
Listing agents, 11, 35–36. See also Real estate agents
Listings

exclusive listings, 197
expired listings, 78
"Make Me Move" listings, 76
Multiple Listing Service, 32, 55
pocket listings, 76
pre-market listings, 77
withdrawn listings, 77–78
Loan approval, 89
Loan officer, 42, 202
Loan origination, 203
Loan origination fee, 205
Loan servicing, 203
Loan-to-value ratio (LTV), 84, 177, 203
Loan types, 100–107, 185
Location considerations, 11, 49, 56–58, 150
Lock-in period, 203
Lock-in rate, 89, 105, 203, 209
Low-income buyers, 81, 106

M

"Magic number," 82–83, 203
Maintenance tasks, 19, 24, 180–182
"Make Me Move" listings, 76
Market fluctuations, 16, 26
Mixed-rate mortgage, 104–105
Money market accounts, 153
"Money pit," 16, 124
Mortgage application, 89, 186
Mortgage banker, 168, 204
Mortgage broker, 168, 204
Mortgage commitment, 90–91
Mortgage definition, 203
Mortgage insurance, 204. See also Private mortgage insurance
Mortgage insurance premium, 204
Mortgage payments
    biweekly mortgage, 188
    credit score and, 25
    mortgage types, 100–107, 185
Mortgage preapproval, 88–109

definition of, 206–207
documents for, 89–91, 93
final approval, 91
importance of, 81, 153
process of, 89–90
tips for, 92
Mortgage types, 100–107, 185
Mortgagee, 204
Moving costs, 20
Multiple Listing Service (MLS), 32, 55
Mutual funds, 153

N

National Association of Realtors (NAR), 38
Networking, 78
New home construction, 75, 192
New home decisions, 18–20
No-cost loan, 205
No-points loan, 205
Note rate, 205
Notes, 205

O

Offer, making, 110–122, 148–149
Open houses, 33, 43, 78
Original principal balance, 205
Origination fee, 205
Owner financing, 206

P

Pets, 27, 58, 63
Pitfalls, avoiding, 16, 147–156
PITI (principal, interest, taxes, insurance), 206
PITI reserves, 206
Planned unit development (PUD), 206
Pocket listings, 76

Points, 108, 195, 205
Pre-market listings, 77
Preapproval, 88–109
definition of, 206–207
documents for, 89–91, 93
final approval, 91
importance of, 81, 153
process of, 89–90
tips for, 92
Prepayment, 207
Prepayment penalty, 207
Prequalification, 89, 153, 207
Previously owned homes, 18–20
Prime rate, 207
Principal, 207
Principal balance, 208
Private mortgage insurance (PMI), 83, 85, 102–103, 107, 177, 208
Professionals, 29–46
advice from, 16–17
benefits of, 20, 29–46, 116–122, 157
duties of, 38–40
finding, 31–37
interviewing, 33
listening to, 16–17
qualities of, 30–31, 38–40
relationship with, 37–46
team of, 29–46
Proof of funds (POF), 114
Property, distressed, 65–79
Property, flipping, 10, 125
Property survey, 159, 210, 1261
Property taxes, 24, 27, 55, 208
Property Virgins, 9, 23
Public auction, 66–69, 208
Purchase agreement, 137, 145, 208.
See also Contract
Purchases, 154, 182–183

R

Rate lock, 89, 105, 203, 209
Real estate agents. *See also* Real
  estate professionals
  benefits of, 29–30
  definition of, 209
  duties of, 38–40
  finding, 31–37
  interviewing, 33
  listing agents, 11, 35–36
  qualities of, 30–31, 38–40
  relationship with, 37–46
  types of, 35–36
Real estate attorney, 20, 116–122, 157
Real estate brokers, 37–40, 189
Real estate bubble, 71, 74–75
Real estate commission, 36–37, 45, 191
Real estate market
  cycles in, 72–75
  fluctuations in, 16, 26
  housing crisis and, 31, 71, 74–75,
    81, 101, 130
  inventory shortages, 73–79
  supply and demand, 72–75, 112
Real estate owned properties, 66
Real estate professionals, 29–46
  advice from, 16–17
  benefits of, 20, 29–46, 116–122, 157
  duties of, 38–40
  finding, 31–37
  interviewing, 33
  listening to, 16–17
  qualities of, 30–31, 38–40
  relationship with, 37–46
  team of, 29–46
Real Estate Settlement Procedures
  Act (RESPA), 209
Real estate team, 29–46. *See also*
  Real estate professionals
Real property, 209
Realtor, 29–37, 209. *See also*

Real estate agents
Rental costs, 21, 26–27
Rental properties, 77, 159
REO properties, 66
Resale value considerations, 5
  6, 125, 150–151
Restrictions, 159, 193
Retirement accounts, 115
Reverse annuity mortgage, 199

S

Sacrifices, making, 14–15, 19
Sales comparisons, 125–126,
  142–143, 192
Savings, 18, 84–85, 93. *See also*
  Down payment
Savings account, 74, 83–84, 93, 115,
  152–154
Second mortgage, 107–109, 209
Seller's agents, 11, 35–36, 209. *See
  also* Real estate agents
Sellers' market, 73–74
Settlement process, 169–177
  attorney for, 157
  closing costs for, 20, 93, 107, 120,
    170, 190
  delays in, 171
  documents for, 170–171
  finalizing, 178
  homeowners insurance for, 169–170,
    173–176
  private mortgage insurance for, 177
  reviewing, 170–171
Shopping tips, 154, 182–183
Short sales, 65–72, 210
Stability, 12, 24, 26, 92–93, 96
Subdivisions, 58, 159, 210
Subprime lending, 101
Supply and demand, 72–75, 112
Surveys, 159, 161, 210

T

Tax breaks, 26
Tax liens, 37, 72, 164, 202, 210
Title, 72, 157–159, 210
Title, chain of, 163, 189
Title, clear, 72, 167, 190
Title clouds, 190
Title company, 157–168, 211
Title examination, 158, 197
Title fees, 20
Title insurance, 157, 161–168, 211
Title search, 158–159, 211
Transfer of ownership, 211
Transfer tax, 211

U

"Under contract," 90, 211
Underwriter, 91, 212
Upside-down properties, 71, 77

V

VA loan, 101–103, 106, 212
Value
   appraised value, 144–145, 187
   assessed value, 187
   fair market value, 197
   loan-to-value ratio, 84, 177, 203
   long-term value, 24–26
   resale value, 56, 125, 150–151
Veterans Administration (VA), 212

W

Walk-through inspection, 170
"Walkaway number," 116
Wealth, building, 9–10, 24–25
Wish lists, 49, 51–54
Withdrawn listings, 77–78